P9-AOM-901

PENGUIN CLASSICS

SELECTED POEMS

MARINA TSVETAEVA was born in Moscow in 1892, the daughter of a pianist and a museum curator. After enjoying a relatively secure and comfortable childhood she published her first poems in 1910, and in 1911 she married fellow poet Sergei Efron. They had two daughters before the Russian revolution broke out, and it was at that time she began to experience the turmoil and brutality of early twentieth-century Russia. During the years of the famine that ensued, she was forced to place her daughters in a State orphanage, where one of them died of malnutrition. Tsvetaeva later followed her husband to Czechoslovakia, where they lived in exile until Efron's return to Russia in 1937. Efron subsequently was arrested, and he died in a labor camp. Tsvetaeva returned to Russia with their son in 1939 but was driven to despair by the difficulty of finding food for the both of them, and, in 1941, she hanged herself. Along with Pasternak, Mandelstam, and Akhmatova, Marina Tsvetaeva stands as one of the four great Russian poets of this century and is one of the most important woman writers in the Western canon.

ELAINE FEINSTEIN is a novelist, poet, and biographer. Her biography of Marina Tsvetaeva, *A Captive Lion*, was published in 1987.

MARINA TSVETAEVA

Selected Poems

Translated and introduced by
ELAINE FEINSTEIN

with literal versions provided by

Angela Livingstone   Simon Franklin
Valentina Coe   Vera Traill
Jana Howlett   Bernard Comrie
Maxwell Shorter   Cathy Porter

PENGUIN BOOKS

PENGUIN BOOKS
Published by the Penguin Group
Penguin Group (USA) Inc., 375 Hudson Street, New York, New York 10014, U.S.A.
Penguin Books Ltd, 80 Strand, London WC2R 0RL, England
Penguin Books Australia Ltd, 250 Camberwell Road, Camberwell, Victoria 3124, Australia
Penguin Books Canada Ltd, 10 Alcorn Avenue, Toronto, Ontario, Canada M4V 3B2
Penguin Books India (P) Ltd, 11 Community Centre, Panchsheel Park, New Delhi – 110 017, India
Penguin Group (NZ), cnr Airborne and Rosedale Roads, Albany, Auckland 1310, New Zealand
Penguin Books (South Africa) (Pty) Ltd, 24 Sturdee Avenue,
Rosebank, Johannesburg 2196, South Africa

Penguin Books Ltd, Registered Offices: 80 Strand, London WC2R 0RL, England

First published in Great Britain by Oxford University Press 1971
Published in the United States of American by
Oxford University Press 1971
Second edition published in Great Britain by
Oxford University Press 1981
Published in the United States of America by
Oxford University Press 1982
Third edition published in Great Britain by
Century Hutchinson Ltd., 1986
Published in the United States of America by E. P. Dutton 1987
This fourth edition published in Great Britain by
Oxford University Press 1993
Published in the United States of America in Penguin Books 1994

9 10

Copyright © Elaine Feinstein 1971, 1981, 1986, 1993
All rights reserved

LIBRARY OF CONGRESS CATALOGING IN PUBLICATION DATA
Tsvetaeva, Marina, 1892–1941.
[Poems. English. Selections]
Selected poems/Marina Tsvetaeva: translated and introduced by Elaine
Feinstein: with literal versions provided by Angela Livingstone . . .
[et al.]—4th ed., rev. and enl.
p.   cm.
Translated from Russian.
1. Tsvetaeva, Marina, 1892–1941—Translations into English.
I. Feinstein, Elaine.   II. Title.
PG3476.T5A257   1993   891.71´42—dc20   93–18717
ISBN 0 14 01.8759 6

Printed in the United States of America

Except in the United States of America, this book is sold subject to the condi-
tion that it shall not, by way of trade or otherwise, be lent, re-sold, hired out,
or otherwise circulated without the publisher's prior consent in any form of
binding or cover other than that in which it is published and without
a similar condition including this condition being imposed
on the subsequent purchaser.

Contents

List of Collaborators

Literal versions of the poems were provided by the following:

Angela Livingstone

I know the truth
What is this gypsy passion for
    separation
We shall not escape Hell
We are keeping an eye on the girls
No one has taken anything away
You throw back your head
Where does this tenderness come
    from?
Bent with worry
Today or tomorrow the snow will
    melt
VERSES ABOUT MOSCOW
From INSOMNIA
POEMS FOR AKHMATOVA
POEMS FOR BLOK
A kiss on the head
Praise to the Rich
The Poet
POEM OF THE END
Epitaph
Homesickness
Readers of Newspapers
When I look at the flight of the
    leaves
From POEMS TO CZECHOSLOVAKIA

Valentina Coe

POEM OF THE MOUNTAIN

Simon Franklin

God help us   Smoke!
Ophelia: in Defence of the Queen

Wherever you are I can reach you
From WIRES
Sahara
Appointment
Rails
You loved me
To Boris Pasternak
From THE RATCATCHER. From
    Chapter 1 and from Chapter 2
Desk
Bus

Vera Traill

From THE RATCATCHER. From
    Children's Paradise

Jana Howlett

From SWANS' ENCAMPMENT

Bernard Comrie

Yesterday he still looked in my eyes

Maxwell Shorter

Some ancestor of mine
I'm glad your sickness
To Mayakovsky
It's not like waiting for post
My ear attends to you
As people listen intently
Strong doesn't mate with strong
In a world
I opened my veins

Cathy Porter

From POEMS TO A SON

Introduction

SOME twenty-five years ago I began to work on translations of Marina Tsvetaeva's poetry, with the generous help of Angela Livingstone of the University of Essex, who provided me with annotated, word-for-word literal versions; this led to the first edition in English of a selection of Tsvetaeva's poems.[1] At that time they existed only in Russian, and although a small Soviet edition appeared in 1965,[2] what she had written in 1933, in exile and neglect, remained close to the truth: 'I went abroad in 1922, and my reader remained in Russia where my poems no longer penetrate ... And thus, I am here without readers; in Russia, without books.'

The present situation is very different. There are five volumes of her work available in Moscow, and many readers in the West who do not know Russian have been drawn to her poetry, now in the hands of several translators. Women poets in particular have been moved by the violence of her emotions and the ferocity of her expression, and have perhaps taken some courage from her obstinacy. Her ruling passion was Poetry, and it came before everything else. She wrote: 'I don't love life as such ... If I were to be taken beyond the ocean, into Paradise, and forbidden to write, I would refuse the ocean and Paradise.' For me, what was so striking about her determination to fulfil the demands of a 'golden, incomparable genius'—to use the words of Boris Pasternak—was that she did so alongside all the responsibilities of womanhood, even though she was impractical, eccentric, and singularly unprepared to look after her small family in a time of crisis.

We know enough about her life now to marvel at the inner strength that sustained her.[3] As a daughter of a Professor of Fine Arts at Moscow University, she spent a childhood of considerable material comfort; but the household was not a happy one. Marina's mother, a talented pianist, was by far the most powerful presence in it; and she died of tuberculosis when Marina was fourteen. After her death, Marina abandoned the study of music her mother had imposed upon her, and began to develop her own precocious gifts. To her mother, nevertheless, she owed that stern indifference to material well-being which was to characterize the rest of her life. 'After a mother like that,' Marina reflected, 'I had only one alternative: to become a poet.'

By the age of eighteen she already had a considerable reputation, and could number the poet Maximilian Voloshin among her friends. It was at Voloshin's dacha in the Crimea that she met Sergei Efron, a seventeen-year-old orphan whose mother and father had been early Revolutionaries. Marina and Sergei were married in 1912; and before war broke out in 1914 were inordinately happy, though it was always clear that Tsvetaeva was the stronger figure. They had two daughters. During the war years, Tsvetaeva had a brief love affair with Osip Mandelstam, and a longer and more intense relationship with the lesbian poet Sofia Parnok, which caused Sergei great distress.

When the Revolution came, Sergei's loyalty to his fellow officers led him to join the White Army; and Tsvetaeva returned to Moscow to collect their children. The total confusion that followed the outbreak of the Civil War, however, prevented her from joining him and they were separated for five years. At the height of the Moscow famine, Tsvetaeva was forced to put both her daughters into a State orphanage: when Alya became ill, she removed her, but the younger daughter, Irina, died there of hunger in the winter of 1919.

In 1922, when Tsvetaeva heard from Erenburg that Efron was alive in Prague, she at once made the decision to join him; and so followed a long period of exile in which she saw her early fame vanish, and learnt to accept growing loneliness and rejection. Her marriage and her many passionate love-affairs were largely ill-fated; her most intense experience of love came to her during the few years she lived in Prague, and she records the ending of that in 'Poem of the Mountain' and 'Poem of the End'. In a letter speaking of the loneliness he then felt, her husband gives a perceptive account of Marina's own dependency on himself: 'I told Marina about my decision that we should separate. For two weeks she was in a state of madness . . . finally she informed me that she was unable to leave me since she was unable to enjoy a moment of peace.'

Tsvetaeva always had to cope with the daily necessities of shopping and cooking in conditions of unremitting poverty, while acting as the only support of her surviving daughter, her son Georgy, born in Vshenory in 1925, and a husband rarely free from tuberculosis. When she was offered the opportunity to earn money through a reading in Paris, she had to beg 'a simple washable dress' from her Czech friend, Anna Teskovà, to replace the woollen one she had been living in all winter. As she wrote in another letter: 'We are devoured by coal, gas, the milkman, the baker . . . the only meat we eat is horsemeat.'

The one central and continuing reality of Tsvetaeva's life was poetry and her loyalty to individual poets, which ran across the political boundaries of that time. So it is not surprising that she did not long hold the enthusiasm of the distinguished group of Russian émigrés who lived in Paris. She always needed the love of friends and the company of poets. And yet there is something inevitable in the way she antagonized the émigrés who had initially welcomed her with honour. As she said in a letter to the Estonian poet, Yuri Ivask, in 1933: 'In the emigration they at first (hotheadedly) publish me, then having come to their senses withdraw me from circulation, having realized that there is something in me that is not theirs: it is from over there.'

They were not altogether mistaken; Tsvetaeva felt a strong allegiance to some poets in Soviet Russia. In 1926, when Efron with two others began the magazine *Vyorsty*, it included Pasternak, Babel, and Yesenin, along with Tsvetaeva. And when the news of Mayakovsky's suicide reached the West, Tsvetaeva refused to sign the notorious émigré letter which read in part: 'Quelles que puissent être les nuances possibles quant a l'appréciation du talent poétique de Maiakovsky, nous, les écrivains russes, mieux informés que les étrangers de la situation actuelle de notre littérature, nous affirmons que Maiakovsky n'a jamais été un grand poète russe . . .'[4] Later she defended Yesenin and

Mayakovsky as poets, against the powerful figure of Bunin, in *Poet o Kritike*, which must have sealed her unpopularity. No wonder she felt, as she wrote in a letter to Anna Teskovà: 'In Paris, with rare personal exceptions, everyone hates me; they write all sorts of nasty things, leave me out in all sorts of ways, and so on.'[5]

Yet the emigration did not only draw away from her on political grounds. They disapproved of her, as Nina Berberova makes clear in her autobiography, *The Italics are Mine*,[6] for her lack of the domestic graces that make poverty bearable. Men of comparable genius often find women to look after them. Tsvetaeva was less fortunate, and she resented the burdens of domesticity. As she wrote to Pasternak in 1935: 'I have been consumed by the daily round . . . I have no time to think . . . I have only ever been myself in my notebooks and on solitary roads (which have been rare) for all my life I have been leading a child by the hand'.[7]

She well recognized the attitude of the émigrés towards her, and for her part disliked the society of the cultivated: 'They don't like poetry,' she once wrote to Pasternak. 'And what am I apart from that, not *poetry* but that from which it is made. An inhospitable hostess, a young woman in an old dress.'[8]

Her happiest time, she came to feel, in spite of the failed love-affair, had been in Prague. There a whole city had been suffused for her with a sense of intense, if painful, vitality. In 1926 she is already writing to Anna Teskovà of her desire to return there: 'In that same Chekhia one can live humanly; I have lived inhumanly and I'm tired of living like that, I'm tired in advance.' She wanted to find some place to live in the centre of the city where it would be possible for her to visit galleries and attend concerts, and enjoy the city's richness without being wholly bound by the need to look after her children. As a poet, she felt her exile bitterly, although unlike Efron, who became a Communist, she was not attracted to the régime. Her daughter Alya, who had been like a sister to her in the Civil War period, began to find it easier to relate to her father. An unpublished letter to Bunin's wife, quoted by Viktoria Schweitzer,[9] shows the bitter isolation Tsvetaeva now endured in her own household: 'S. and Alya shut themselves away from me in the kitchen and begin to talk in hushed voices.'

When she returned to Russia with her son in 1939 (following Efron, who had been exposed in 1937 as a Soviet agent), she and her family were suspected of working against the Soviet government. Alya was arrested two months after her mother's arrival, and Sergei himself a month later. When war came Marina was evacuated with Georgy to Yelabuga. There in 1941 she hanged herself. And yet Marina Tsvetaeva was a woman who had 'always loved life so much', as Anna Teskovà wrote when the news of her death reached her.

She must have been a difficult and probably over-demanding person; many speak of the antagonism she aroused in them, though it is clear that she also made enduring friendships. Osip Mandelstam, to whom she offers 'Moscow' in a sequence of poems in 1916, was in love with her for a time and dedicated a number of his poems to her. Many of her most intense and valued relationships took place at a distance, through letters. From her side, she offered a homage approaching awe to the barely-known figure of Alexander Blok, who embodied for her what she felt to be the essentially supernatural quality of poetry itself. In the same spirit, she entered in the summer of 1925 into an intense correspondence with Rainer Maria Rilke, whom she was never to meet.[10] Above all, Boris Pasternak, whom she met seldom after 1918, sustained her by letters of admiration throughout her exile.

Tsvetaeva spoke of poetry as Emily Dickinson did in the famous letter to a bewildered Higginson: 'If I read a book and it makes my whole body so cold I know no fire can ever warm me, I know that is poetry. If I feel physically as if the top of my head were taken off, I know that is poetry. These are the only ways I know it. Is there any other way?' There were many other ways current in Tsvetaeva's time, and most of them were concerned with putting poetry to the service of social or political good. For Tsvetaeva essentially the true poet could never do anything so willed, since she was the victim of a kind of visitation. In 'Art in the Light of Conscience' she declared: 'Blok wrote *The Twelve* in a single night, and got up in complete exhaustion, like one who has been driven upon.'[11] For 'the condition of creation' was for her analogous to dreaming, when 'suddenly obeying an unknown necessity, you set fire to a house or push your friend down from the mountain top'. The least egotistical of poets, though so many of her greater poems arose from her own pain, she preserved what to her was the essential demand of poetry: 'To let the ear hear, the hand race (and when it doesn't race—to stop)', and you can sense that abandonment of self in the very movement of her lines, in their onward, compelled, flow.

Tsvetaeva was a warm admirer of Anna Akhmatova, to whom she wrote several poems, and inevitably their names occur together in any account of the poetry of the period. As Max Hayward said in his Foreword to the 1st edition of these translations:

> Marina Tsvetaeva's unflinching integrity in the employment of her genius puts her among the small band of Russian poet-witnesses who felt themselves to be, and recognized in each other the voices of the country and the keepers of its values during what Blok called the 'terrible years'. There were only four of them—besides Tsvetaeva: Pasternak, Akhmatova, and Mandelstam. The last of them to die was Akhmatova, who, towards the end of her life, in 1961, wrote about them all in a remarkable poem entitled quite simply: 'There are four of us':

> > On paths of air I seem to overhear
> > two friends, two voices, talking in their turn.
> >
> > Did I say two? . . . There by the eastern wall,
> > where criss-cross shoots of brambles trail,
> > —O look!—that fresh dark elderberry branch
> > is like a letter from Marina in the mail.[12]
> >
> > > November 1961 (in delirium)

The two women were very different creatures. Tsvetaeva never enjoyed a string of admirers as Akhmatova did; nor did she perceive herself as a beautiful woman. When she was young she thought herself too healthy-looking to be romantic; when life had worn her down she knew she often looked far older than her years. She once remarked scornfully that although she would be the most important woman in all her friends' memoirs, 'she had never counted in the masculine present'. She loved Konstantin Rodzevitch—the 'hero' of 'Poem of the End'—just because he responded to her as a woman: 'For the person who loves me the woman in me is a gift; but the person who loves *her* creates a debt I can never repay.' After her affair with Rodzevitch ended she wrote poignantly to her friend Bakhrakh: 'To be loved is something of which I have not mastered the art . . .'[13] Yet Tsvetaeva had her own sense of grandeur. She knew herself to belong to the finest poets of her century.

Talking about Rilke, Tsvetaeva spoke of poems as prayer, but she did not make the mistake of blurring the distinction between poetry and religion, any more than she would ever allow for poetry the utilitarian hope that Art can do civic good. Both were as much limitations she recognized in poetry, as magniloquent claims made for it. In the closing passage from 'Art in the Light of Conscience' she makes that clear: 'To be a human being is more important, because it is more needed . . . The doctor and the priest are humanly more important, all the others are socially more important.'

It is in what Tsvetaeva's poetry includes that we sense its greatness; there is no censor between her and her experience, nothing that checks what is given to her from finding its shape upon the page. And she understood very well the ambiguous relationship she took up to the world of daily living. There is nothing wilful in this; it is simply the other side of the truth she records sadly and honestly, in another letter. 'Externally, things always go badly with me, because I don't love it (the external), I take no account of it, I don't give it the required importance and demand *nothing* from it. Everything I love changes from an external thing into an inward one, from the moment of my love, it stops being external.'[14] She takes no pride in this, though as she makes clear at the conclusion of 'Art in the Light of

Conscience' she 'would not exchange her work for any other. Aware of greater things, I do lesser ones, this is why there is no forgiveness for me. Only such as I will be held responsible at the Judgement of Conscience. But if there is a Judgement Day of the word, at that I am guiltless.'

It was with a sense of some temerity, as well as enormous excitement, that I began to try and find an English poetic equivalent for her eccentric Russian genius. All translation is difficult; Tsvetaeva is a particularly difficult poet. No line by line version could catch her passionate, onward flow. And her pauses and sudden changes of speed were felt always against the deliberate constraint of the forms she had chosen. Perhaps the exact metres could not be kept, but some sense of her shapeliness, as well as her roughness, had to survive.

For this reason I have invariably followed her stanzaic patterning, though I have frequently indented lines where she does not. This slight shift is one of many designed to dispel any sense of static solidity, which blocks of lines convey to an English eye, and which is not induced by the Russian.

There were other structural changes. It was impossible to preserve all her startling distortions of word order, in an uninflected language like English, without dangerously confusing the reader. Some repetitions had to be sacrificed to preserve the pattern of her rhythms. The very compactness of Russian and its polysyllabic structure were severe problems, the more harrowing because she makes such brilliant use of them. Sometimes, so that a poem could move forward in a natural English syntax, connective words had to be introduced, and in the process, and against my will, I observed that some of her abruptness had been smoothed out, and the poem had gained a different, more logical scheme of development. There were other problems. Tsvetaeva's punctuation is strongly individual; but to have reproduced it pedantically would often have destroyed the tone of the English version. In my first drafts I experimented with using extra word space, but usually then restored Tsvetaeva's dash—at least in the early poems; in later poems a space has often seemed closer to the movement of her lines. Dashes that indicate the beginning of direct speech are retained. I frequently left out exclamation marks where their presence seemed to weaken a line that was already loud and vibrant. Furthermore, there were difficulties of diction. Words with echoes of ancient folk-songs and the Bible were particularly hard to carry across into English.

Although, as I think of these specific problems, I am not sure how far a discussion of methods of translation attracts much useful reflection, some word seems necessary, especially since I have worked with different linguists. Some of the poems, such as 'Poem of the End', as Angela Livingstone describes in her detailed note, were transliterated into English, as well as written out in word-for-word literal versions, which indicated, by hyphenation, words which were represented by a single Russian word. Other poems, such as the 'Insomnia' cycle and 'Verses about Moscow', also prepared for me by Angela Livingstone, were first read on to tape in Russian; and then (on the same tape) as literal versions which I wrote out myself and used alongside the printed Russian text. For 'An Attempt at Jealousy' I used the literal prose version at the foot of the page in the *Penguin Book of Russian Verse*. Both Angela Livingstone and Valentina Coe were prepared to help with intractable problems of Russian meanings throughout that 1st edition. For the 1981 edition, Simon Franklin produced written literal versions very much as Angela Livingstone had done, though without transliterations; and he too gave full indications of changes of rhythm, musical stress, and word-play in his notes.

I am not sure how much this bears upon what Octavio Paz called the 'transformation' of a poem from one language to another. Poems are not translated *consistently*. Every line proposes a new set of possibilities. And with a poet such as Tsvetaeva, whose movement extends through many stanzas, the process was often a matter of reading towards every problematic line again and again from the opening of the English version, to be sure the total movement had been sustained. I do not pretend to understand why occasionally a translator will suddenly have the sense of writing the poem itself, freshly, as though for the first time, while on other occasions every painstaking draft appears to die under the hand. When the transformation altogether refused to happen, regretfully the poem had to be left out of the selection.

The poems are arranged in order of their (original) composition, with the more recent translations fitted into the chronology. Chronological order is particularly important for an understanding of many of the poems, notably 'Bus', for instance, where Tsvetaeva's inner weariness is unmistakable, even though her technical virtuosity is unimpaired. The annotation is based on Angela Livingstone's notes to the 1st edition, or added where necessary for later translations. In choosing more poems I have tried to represent a wider range of Tsvetaeva's work, even if, as in 'The Ratcatcher' (an hundred-page narrative poem of incomparable exuberance), only short extracts were feasible.

The collaborators are listed in full, but I should like to acknowledge further Angela Livingstone's generous collaboration for the 1st edition; and Valentina Coe, who made a literal version of 'Poem of the Mountain'. I should also like to thank Bernard Comrie, Jana Howlett, Vera Traill, Leslie Milne, and Dr Nikolai Andreyev. I want to mention particularly Masha Enzensberger whose sad death in 1992 was a great personal loss to me, and whose help in reading and understanding Tsvetaeva over the years has been indispensable. I should like to thank Simon Franklin for his annotated word-for-word translations for the 2nd edition; and Maxwell Shorter and Cathy Porter who made literal versions for the ten new lyrics in this volume. I should also like to thank Anthony Rudolph of Menard Press and Peter Baldwin of Delos Press who brought out a small pamphlet, *Black Earth*, which included most of the new poems in this edition.

Elaine Feinstein
London, 1992

1 *Selected Poems of Marina Tsvetayeva*, tr. Elaine Feinstein (Oxford University Press, 1971); Paperback enlarged edition (OUP, 1981); 3rd edition reissued (Hutchinson, 1986); the present, further enlarged edition, with revised introduction (Oxford Poets, and Penguin USA, 1993).

2 Marina Tsvetaeva, *Izbrannaye proizvedeniya* (Moscow–Leningrad, 1965). Also a volume of her poems published in Munich: *Lebediny stan. Stikhi, 1917–1921*, ed. Gleb Struve (1957).

3 Several biographies, editions of letters, and translations of her prose have appeared: Simon Karlinsky, *Marina Cvetaeva—Her Life and Art* (Berkeley and Los Angeles, 1966); *A Captive Spirit: Selected Prose of Marina Tsvetayeva*, ed. and tr. Janet Marin King (Ann Arbor, 1989); *Tsvetayeva: A Pictorial Biography*, ed. with an introduction Carl Proffer (Ann Arbor, 1981); Simon Karlinsky, *Marina Cvetaeva, The Woman, Her World and Her Poetry* (Cambridge, 1985); Elaine Feinstein, *A Captive Lion* (London, 1986); *Letters Summer 1926: Letters between Tsvetayeva, Pasternak and Rilke*, ed. Yevgeny Pasternak, Yelena Pasternak, and Konstantin M. Azadovsky (London, 1986; Oxford Paperbacks, 1988); Viktoria Schweitzer, *Tsvetaeva* (London, 1992).

4 'Autour de Mayakovsky', *Les Nouvelles Littéraires* (Paris, 12 July, 1930).

5 Letter no. 31, Meudon, Easter, 1927. Marina Tsvetaeva, *Pis'ma Anne Teskovoi (Letters to Anna Teskovà)*, (Academia Praha, Prague, 1969).

6 Nina Berberova, *The Italics are Mine* (New York, 1969).

7 Letter from Tsvetaeva to Pasternak, late October, 1935, *Novy Mir* 4, 1969.

8 Letter from Tsvetaeva to Pasternak, 19 July 1925, *Neizdannye Pis'ma*, ed. Gleb and Nikita Struve (Paris, 1972).

9 Viktoria Schweitzer, *Tsvetaeva* (ibid.), p. 320.

10 *Letters Summer 1926* (ibid.).

11 All quotations from 'Art in the Light of Conscience' are taken from the translation by Angela Livingstone and Valentina Coe in *Modern Russian Poets on Poetry* (Ardis Press, 1974, pp. 145–84).

12 *Poems of Akhmatova*, tr. Kunitz and Hayward (London, 1974).

13 Letter to Bakhrakh, 29 September 1923 *Mosty* (Munich, 1960, vol. 5).

14 Letter to Anna Teskovà, 30 December 1925 (ibid.).

POEMS

I know the truth

I know the truth—give up all other truths!
No need for people anywhere on earth to struggle.
Look—it is evening, look, it is nearly night:
what do you speak of, poets, lovers, generals?

The wind is level now, the earth is wet with dew,
the storm of stars in the sky will turn to quiet.
And soon all of us will sleep under the earth, we
who never let each other sleep above it.

1915

What is this gypsy passion for separation

What is this gypsy passion for separation, this
   readiness to rush off—when we've just met?
My head rests in my hands as I
   realize, looking into the night

that no one turning over our letters has
   yet understood how completely and
how deeply faithless we are, which is
   to say: how true we are to ourselves.

1915

We shall not escape Hell

We shall not escape Hell, my passionate
sisters, we shall drink black resins—
we who sang our praises to the Lord
with every one of our sinews, even the finest,

we did not lean over cradles or
spinning wheels at night, and now we are
carried off by an unsteady boat
under the skirts of a sleeveless cloak,

we dressed every morning in
fine Chinese silk, and we would
sing our paradisal songs at
the fire of the robbers' camp,

slovenly needlewomen, (all
our sewing came apart), dancers,
players upon pipes: we have been
the queens of the whole world!

first scarcely covered by rags,
then with constellations in our hair, in
gaol and at feasts we have
bartered away heaven,

in starry nights, in the apple
orchards of Paradise.
—Gentle girls, my beloved sisters,
we shall certainly find ourselves in Hell!

1915

Some ancestor of mine

Some ancestor of mine was a violinist
  and a thief into the bargain.
Does this explain my vagrant disposition
  and hair that smells of the wind?

Dark, curly-haired, hooknosed, he is
  the one who steals apricots
from the cart, using my hand. Yes,
  he is responsible for my fate.

Admiring the ploughman at his labour,
  he used to twirl a dog rose
in his lips. He was always unreliable
  as a friend, but a tender lover.

Fond of his pipe, the moon, beads, and all
  the young women in the neighbourhood . . .
I think he may have also been a coward,
  my yellow-eyed ancestor.

His soul was sold for a farthing,
  so he did not walk at midnight
in the cemetery. He may have worn
  a knife tucked in his boot.

Perhaps he pounced round corners
  like a sinuous cat.
I wonder suddenly: did
  he even play the violin?

I know nothing mattered to him
  any more than last year's snow.
That's what he was like, my ancestor.
  And that's the kind of poet I am.

1915

I'm glad your sickness

I'm glad your sickness is not caused by me.
Mine is not caused by you. I'm glad to know
the heavy earth will never flow away
from us, beneath our feet, and so
we can relax together, and not watch
our words. When our sleeves touch
we shall not drown in waves of rising blush.

I'm glad to see you calmly now embrace
another girl in front of me, without
any wish to cause me pain, as you
don't burn if I kiss someone else.
I know you never use my tender name,
my tender spirit, day or night. And
no one in the silence of a church
will sing their Hallelujahs over us.

Thank you for loving me like this,
for you feel love, although you do not know it.
Thank you for the nights I've spent in quiet.
Thank you for the walks under the moon
you've spared me and those sunset meetings unshared.
Thank you. The sun will never bless our heads.
Take my sad thanks for this: you do not cause
my sickness. And I don't cause yours.

1915

We are keeping an eye on the girls

We are keeping an eye on the girls, so that the *kvass*
doesn't go sour in the jug, or the pancakes cold,
counting over the rings, and pouring Anis
into the long bottles with their narrow throats,

straightening tow thread for the peasant woman:
filling the house with the fresh smoke of
incense   and we are sailing over Cathedral square
arm in arm with our godfather, silks thundering.

The wet nurse has a screeching cockerel
in her apron—her clothes are like the night.
She announces in an ancient whisper that
a dead young man   lies in the chapel.

And an incense cloud wraps the corners
under its own saddened chasuble.
The apple trees are white, like angels—and
the pigeons on them—grey—like incense itself.

And the pilgrim woman sipping *kvass* from the ladle
on the edge of the couch, is telling
to the very end a tale about Razin
and his most beautiful Persian girl.

1916

No one has taken anything away

No one has taken anything away—
   there is even a sweetness for me in being apart.
I kiss you now across the many
   hundreds of miles that separate us.

I know: our gifts are unequal, which is
   why my voice is—quiet, for the first time.
What can my untutored verse
   matter to you, a young Derzhavin?

For your terrible flight I give you blessing.
   Fly, then, young eagle! You
have stared into the sun without blinking.
   Can my young gaze be too heavy for you?

No one has ever stared more
   tenderly or more fixedly after you . . .
I kiss you—across hundreds of
   separating years.

                                    1916

You throw back your head

You throw back your head, because
you are proud. And a braggart.
This February has
brought me a gay companion!

Clattering with gold pieces, and
slowly puffing out smoke, we
walk like solemn foreigners
throughout my native city.

And whose attentive hands have
touched your eyelashes, beautiful boy, and
when or how many times your
lips have been kissed

I do not ask. That dream my thirsty
spirit has conquered. Now
I can honour in you the
divine boy, ten years old!

Let us wait by the river that
rinses the coloured beads of street-lights:
I shall take you as far as the square
that has witnessed adolescent Tsars.

Whistle out your boyish
pain, your heart squeezed in your hand.
My indifferent and crazy creature—
now set free—goodbye!

1916

Where does this tenderness come from?

Where does this tenderness come from?
These are not the—first curls I
have stroked slowly—and lips I
have known are—darker than yours

as stars rise often and go out again
(where does this tenderness come from?)
so many eyes have risen and died out
    in front of these eyes of mine.

and yet no such song have
I heard in the darkness of night before,
(where does this tenderness come from?):
    here, on the ribs of the singer.

Where does this tenderness come from?
And what shall I do with it, young
sly singer, just passing by?
Your lashes are—longer than anyone's.

1916

Bent with worry

Bent with worry, God
    paused, to smile.
And look, there were many
holy angels with bodies of

the radiance he had
    given them,
some with enormous wings and
others without any,

which is why I weep
    so much
because even more than God
himself I love his fair angels.

1916

Today or tomorrow the snow will melt

Today or tomorrow the snow will melt.
You lie alone beneath an enormous fur.
Shall I pity you? Your lips
have gone dry for ever.

Your drinking is difficult, your step heavy.
Every passer-by hurries away from you.
Was it with fingers like yours that Rogozhin
clutched the garden knife?

And the eyes, the eyes in your face!
Two circles of charcoal, year-old circles!
Surely when you were still young your girl
lured you into a joyless house.

Far away—in the night—over asphalt—a cane.
Doors—swing open into—night—under beating wind.
Come in! Appear! Undesired guest! Into
my chamber which is—most bright!

1916

VERSES ABOUT MOSCOW

There are clouds—about us
and domes—about us:
over the whole of Moscow
so many hands are needed!
I lift you up like a
sapling, my best burden: for
to me you are   weightless.

In this city of wonder
this peaceful city
I shall be joyful, even
when I am dead. You
shall reign, or grieve
or perhaps receive my crown:
for you are my first born!

When you fast—in Lent
do not blacken your brows
and honour the churches—these
forty times forty—go
about on foot—stride youthfully
over the whole seven of
these untrammelled hills.

Your turn will come.
You will give Moscow
with tender bitterness
to your daughter also.

As for me—unbroken sleep
and the sound of bells
in the surly dawn of
the Vagankovo cemetery.

Strange and beautiful brother—take this
city no hands built—out of my hands!

Church by church—all the forty times forty, and
the small pigeons also that rise over them.

Take the Spassky gate, with its flowers, where
the orthodox remove their caps, and

the chapel of stars, that refuge from evil,
where the floor is—polished by kisses.

Take from me the incomparable circle
of five cathedrals, ancient, holy friend!

I shall lead you as a guest from another
country to the Chapel of the Inadvertent Joy

where pure gold domes will begin to shine
for you, and sleepless bells will start thundering.

There the Mother of God will drop her
cloak upon you from the crimson clouds

and you will rise up filled with wonderful powers.
Then, you will not repent that you have loved me!

Over the city that great Peter rejected
rolls out the thunder of the bells.

A thundering surf has overturned upon
this woman you have now rejected.

I offer homage to Peter and you also,
yet above you both the bells remain

and while they thunder from that blueness, the
primacy of Moscow cannot be questioned

for all the forty times forty churches
laugh above the arrogance of Tsars.

7

There are seven hills—like seven bells,
seven bells, seven bell-towers. Every
one of the forty times forty churches, and the
seven hills of bells have been numbered.

On a day of bells I was born, it was
the golden day of John the Divine.
The house was gingerbread surrounded by
wattle-fence, and small churches with gold heads.

And I loved it, I loved the first ringing,
the nuns flowing towards Mass, and
the wailing in the stone, the heat of sleeping—
the sense of a soothsayer in the neighbouring house.

Come with me, people of Moscow, all of you,
imbecile, thieving, flagellant mob!
And priest: stop my mouth up firmly
with Moscow—which is a land of bells!

8

Moscow, what a vast
hostelry is your house!
Everyone in Russia is—homeless,
we shall all make our way towards you.

With shameful brands on our backs and
knives—stuck in the tops of our boots,
for you call us in to you
however far away we are,

because for the brand of the criminal
and for every known sickness
we have our healer here,
the Child Panteleimon.

Behind a small door where
people pour in their crowds
lies the Iversky heart—
red-gold and radiant

and a Hallelujah floods
over the burnished fields.
Moscow soil, I bend to
kiss your breast.

1916

From INSOMNIA

2

As I love to
   kiss hands, and
to name everything, I
   love to open
doors!
    Wide—into the night!

Pressing my head
   as I listen to some
heavy step grow softer
   or the wind shaking
the sleepy and sleepless
   woods.

Ah, night
   small rivers of water rise
and bend towards—sleep.
   (I am nearly sleeping.)
Somewhere in the night a
   human being is drowning.

3

In my enormous city it is—night,
as from my sleeping house I go—out,
and people think perhaps I'm a daughter or wife
but in my mind is one thought only: night.

The July wind now sweeps a way for—me.
From somewhere, some window, music though—faint.
The wind can blow until the dawn—today,
in through the fine walls of the breast rib-cage.

Black poplars, windows, filled with—light.
Music from high buildings, in my hand a flower.
Look at my steps—following—nobody.
Look at my shadow, nothing's here of me.

The lights—are like threads of golden beads
in my mouth is the taste of the night—leaf.
Liberate me from the bonds of—day,
my friends, understand: I'm nothing but your dream.

5

Now as a guest from heaven, I
    visit your country:
I have seen the vigil of the forests
    and sleep in the fields.

Somewhere in the night horseshoes
    have torn up the grass, and
there are cows breathing heavily in
    a sleepy cowshed.

Now let me tell you sadly and
    with tenderness of the
goose-watchman awake, and
    the sleeping geese,

of hands immersed in dog's wool,
    grey hair—a grey dog—
and how towards six
    the dawn is beginning.

Tonight—I am alone in the night,
   a homeless and sleepless nun!
Tonight I hold all the keys to this
   the only capital city

and lack of sleep guides me on my path.
   You are so lovely, my dusky Kremlin!
Tonight I put my lips to the breast
   of the whole round and warring earth.

Now I feel hair—like fur—standing on end:
   the stifling wind blows straight into my soul.
Tonight I feel compassion for everyone,
   those who are pitied, along with those who are kissed.

7

   In the pine-tree, tenderly tenderly,
      finely finely: something hissed.
   It is a child with black
      eyes that I see in my sleep.

   From the fair pine-trees hot
      resin drips, and in this
   splendid night there are
      saw-teeth going over my heart.

8

Black as—the centre of an eye, the centre, a blackness
that sucks at light. I love your vigilance

Night, first mother of songs, give me the voice to sing of you
in those fingers lies the bridle of the four winds.

Crying out, offering words of homage to you, I am
only a shell where the ocean is still sounding.

But I have looked too long into human eyes.
Reduce me now to ashes—Night, like a black sun.

9

Who sleeps at night? No one is sleeping.
   In the cradle a child is screaming.
An old man sits over his death, and anyone
   young enough talks to his love, breathes
into her lips, looks into her eyes.

Once asleep—who knows if we'll wake again?
We have time, we have time, we have time to sleep!

From house to house the sharp-eyed
   watchman goes with his pink lantern
and over the pillow scatters the rattle
   of his loud clapper, rumbling.

Don't sleep! Be firm! Listen, the alternative
is—everlasting sleep. Your—everlasting house!

10

Here's another window
with more sleepless people!
Perhaps—drinking wine or
perhaps only sitting,
or maybe two lovers are
unable to part hands.
Every house has
a window like this.

A window at night: cries
of meeting or leaving.
Perhaps—there are many lights,
perhaps—only three candles.
But there is no peace in
my mind anywhere, for
in my house also, these
things are beginning:

Pray for the wakeful house,
friend, and the lit window.

1916

POEMS FOR AKHMATOVA

1

Muse of lament, you are the most beautiful of
    all muses, a crazy emanation of white night:
and you have sent a black snow storm over all Russia.
    We are pierced with the arrows of your cries

so that we shy like horses at the muffled
    many times uttered pledge—Ah!—Anna
Akhmatova—the name is a vast sigh
and it falls into depths without name

and we wear crowns only through stamping
    the same earth as you, with the same sky over us.
Whoever shares the pain of your deathly power will
    lie down immortal—upon his death bed.

In my melodious town the domes are burning
    and the blind wanderer praises our shining Lord.
I give you my town of many bells,
    Akhmatova, and with the gift: my heart.

2

I stand   head in my hands   thinking how
  unimportant are the traps we set for one another
I hold my head in my hands   as I sing
  in this late hour, in the late dawn.

Ah how violent is this wave which has
  lifted me up on to its crest: I sing
of one   that is unique among us
  as the moon is   alone in the sky,

that has flown into my heart like a raven,
  has speared into the clouds
hook-nosed, with deathly anger: even
  your favour is   dangerous,

for you have spread out your night
  over the pure gold of my Kremlin itself
and have tightened my throat with the pleasure
  of singing   as if with a strap.

Yes, I am happy, the dawn never
  burnt with more purity, I am
happy to give everything to you
  and to go away   like a beggar,

for I was the first to give you—
  whose voice   deep darkness!   has
constricted the movement of my breathing—
  the name of the Tsarskoselsky Muse.

3

I am a convict. You won't fall behind.
You are my guard. Our fate is therefore one.
And in that emptiness that we both share
the same command to ride away is given.

And now my demeanour is calm.
And now   my eyes are without guile.
Won't you set me free, my guard, and
let me walk now, towards that pine-tree?

4

You block out everything, even the sun
    at its highest, hold all the stars in your hand!
If only through—some wide open door, I
    could blow like the wind to where you are,

and starting to stammer, suddenly blushing,
    could lower my eyes before you
and fall quiet, in tears, as
    a child sobs to receive forgiveness.

1916

POEMS FOR BLOK

1

Your name is a—bird in my hand
a piece of—ice on the tongue
one single movement of the lips.
Your name is: five signs,
a ball caught in flight, a
silver bell in the mouth

a stone, cast in a quiet pool
makes the splash of your name, and
the sound is in the clatter of
night hooves, loud as a thunderclap
or it speaks straight into my forehead,
shrill as the click of a cocked gun.

Your name—how impossible, it
is a kiss in the eyes on
motionless eyelashes, chill and sweet.
Your name is a kiss of snow
a gulp of icy spring water, blue
as a dove. About your name is: sleep.

1916

2

Tender—spectre
blameless as a knight, who
has called you into
my adolescent life?

In blue dark, grey
and priestly, you
stand here, dressed in snow.

And it's not the wind
that drives me through the town now.
No, this is the third
night I felt the old enemy.

With light blue eyes his
magic has bound
me, that snowy singer:

swan of snow, under
my feet he spreads his feathers.
Hovering feathers,
slowly they dip in the snow.

Thus upon feathers
I go, towards the door
behind which is: death.

He sings to me
behind the blue windows.
He sings to me
as jewelled bells.

Long is the shout from
his swan's beak as
he calls.

Dear spectre of
mist I know this is dreaming,
so one favour now, do
for me, amen: of dispersing.
Amen, amen.

1916

27

You are going—west of the sun now.
You will see there—evening light.
You are going—west of the sun and
snow will cover up your tracks.

Past my windows—passionless
you are going in quiet snow.
Saint of God, beautiful, you
are the quiet light of my soul

but I do not long for your spirit.
Your way is indestructible.
And your hand is pale from holy
kisses, no nail of mine.

By your name I shall not call you.
My hands shall not stretch after you
to your holy waxen face I shall
only bow—from afar

standing under the slow falling snow, I shall
fall to my knees—in the snow.
In your holy name I shall only
kiss that evening snow

where, with majestic pace you
go by in tomb-like quiet,
the light of quiet—holy glory
of it: Keeper of my soul.

1916

At home in Moscow—where the domes are burning,
at home in Moscow—in the sound of bells,
where I live the tombs—in their rows are standing
and in them Tsaritsas—are asleep and Tsars.

And you don't know how—at dawn the Kremlin is
the easiest place to—breathe in the whole wide earth
and you don't know when—dawn reaches the Kremlin
I pray to you until—the next day comes

and I go with you—by your river Neva
even while beside—the Moscow river
I am standing here—with my head lowered
and the line of street lights—sticks fast together.

With my insomnia—I love you wholly.
With my insomnia—I listen for you,
just at the hour throughout—the Kremlin, men
who ring the bells—begin to waken.

Still my river—and your river
still my hand—and your hand
will never join, or not until
one dawn catches up another dawning.

1916

8

And the gadflies gather about indifferent cart-horses,
the red calico of Kaluga puffs out in the wind,
it is a time of whistling quails and huge skies,
bells waving over waves of corn, and more
talk about Germans than anyone can bear.
Now yellow, yellow, beyond the blue trees is a
cross, and a sweet fever, a radiance over
everything: your name   sounding like *angel*.

1916

9

A weak shaft of light through the blackness of hell is
your voice under the rumble of exploding shells

in that thunder like a seraph he is announcing
in a toneless voice, from somewhere else, some

ancient misty morning he inhabits, how he
loved us, who are blind and nameless   who

share the blue cloak of   sinful treachery
and more tenderly than anyone loved the woman who

sank more daringly than any into the night   of evil,
and of his love for you, Russia, which he cannot end.

And he draws an absent-minded finger along
his temple   all the time he tells us of

the days that wait for us, how God will deceive us.
We shall call for the sun and it will not rise.

He spoke like a solitary prisoner
(or perhaps a child speaking to himself)

so that over the whole square the sacred
heart of Alexander Blok appeared to us.

1920

6

Thinking him   human   they
decided to kill him, and
now he's dead. For ever.
—Weep. For the dead angel.

At the day's setting, he
sang the evening beauty.
Three waxen lights now
shudder superstitiously

and lines of light, hot
strings across the snow come from him.
Three waxen candles.
To the sun. The light-bearer.

O now look how
dark his eyelids are fallen,
O now look how
his wings are broken.

The black reciter reads.
The people idly stamp.
Dead lies the singer, and
celebrates resurrection.

1916

10

Look there he is, weary from foreign parts,
a leader without body-guard

there—he is drinking a mountain stream from his hands
a prince without native land.

He has everything in his holy princedom there
Army, bread and mother.

Lovely is your inheritance.
Govern, friend without friends.

1921

A kiss on the head

A kiss on the head—wipes away misery.
I kiss your head.

A kiss on the eyes—takes away sleeplessness.
I kiss your eyes.

A kiss on the lips—quenches the deepest thirst.
I kiss your lips.

A kiss on the head—wipes away memory.
I kiss your head.

1917

From SWANS' ENCAMPMENT

Little mushroom, white Bolitus,
                    my own favourite
The field sways, a chant of Rus'
                    rises over it.
Help me, I'm unsteady on my feet.
This blood-red is making my eyes foggy.

On either side, mouths lie
open and bleeding, and from
each wound rises a cry:
—Mother!

One word is all I hear, as
I stand dazed. From someone
else's womb   into my own:
—Mother!

They all lie in a row,
no line between them,
I recognize that each one was a soldier.
But which is mine? Which one is another's?

This man was White   now he's become Red.
Blood has reddened him.
This one was Red   now he's become White.
Death has whitened him.

—What are you? White?—Can't understand!
                    —Lean on your arm!
Have you been with the Reds?
                    —Ry   -azan.

And so from right and left
Behind   ahead
together, White and Red, one cry of
—Mother!

Without choice. Without anger.
One long moan. Stubbornly.
A cry that reaches up to heaven,
—Mother!

1917–21

Yesterday he still looked in my eyes

Yesterday he still looked in my eyes, yet
    today   his looks are bent aside.   Yesterday
he sat here until the birds began, but
    today   all those larks are   ravens.

Stupid creature! And you are wise, you
    live while I am stunned.
Now for the lament of women in all times:
—My love, what was it I did to you?

And tears are   water, blood is   water,
    a woman always washes in blood and tears.
Love is a step-mother, and no mother:
    then expect no justice or mercy from her.

Ships carry away the ones we love.
    Along the white road they are taken away.
And one cry stretches across the earth:
    —My love, what was it I did to you?

Yesterday he lay at my feet. He even
    compared me with the Chinese empire! Then
suddenly he let his hands fall open, and
    my life fell out like   a rusty kopeck.

A child-murderer, before some court
    I stand   loathsome and timid I am.
And yet even in Hell I shall demand:
    —My love, what was it I did to you?

I ask this chair, I ask the bed: Why?
    Why do I suffer and live in penury?
His kisses stopped. He wanted to break you.
    To kiss another girl is their reply.

He taught me to live in fire, he threw me there,
   and then abandoned me on steppes of ice.
My love, I know what you have done to me.
   —My love, what was it I did to you?

I know everything, don't argue with me!
   I can see now, I'm a lover no longer.
And now I know wherever love holds power
   Death approaches soon   like a gardener.

It is almost like shaking a tree, in time
   some ripe apple comes falling down. So
for everything, for everything   forgive me,
   —my love   whatever it was I did to you.

1920

To Mayakovsky

High above cross and trumpet
baptised in smoke and fire
my clumsy-footed angel—
Hello there, Vladimir!

Carter and horse at once
justice and whim together.
He used to spit on his palms—
Hold on, carthorse of glory!

Singer of gutter miracles,
grubby, arrogant friend—
Hullo there, you who prefer
topaz to diamond!

Now yawn, play your trump card
my thunderbolt of cobbles,
and rake this horse's shaft
once more with your angel wing.

1921

Praise to the Rich

And so, making clear in advance
I know there are miles   between us;
and I reckon myself with the tramps, which
is a place of honour in this world:

under the wheels of luxury, at
table with cripples and hunchbacks ...
From the top of the bell-tower roof,
I proclaim it: I *love* the rich.

For their rotten, unsteady root
for the damage done in their cradle
for the absent-minded way their hands
go in and out of their pockets;

for the way their softest word is
obeyed like a shouted order; because
they will not be let into heaven; and
because they don't look in your eyes;

and because they send secrets   by courier!
and their passions   by errand boy.
In the nights that are thrust upon them they
kiss and drink under compulsion,

and because in all their accountings
in boredom, in gilding, in wadding,
they can't buy me   I'm too brazen:
I confirm it, I *love* the rich!

and in spite of their shaven fatness,
their fine drink   (wink, and spend):
some sudden   defeatedness
and a look that is like a dog's

doubting . . .

the core of their balance
nought, but are the weights true?
I say that among all outcasts
there are no such orphans on earth.

There is also a nasty fable
about camels getting through needles
for that look, surprised to death
apologizing for sickness, as

if they were suddenly bankrupt: 'I would have been
glad to lend, but'   and their silence.
'I counted in carats once and then I was one of them.'
For all these things, I swear it: I *love* the rich.

1922

God help us   Smoke!

God help us   Smoke!
—Forget that. Look at the damp.
These are the ordinary fears
    of anyone moving house

approaching a poor lamp
    for students in miserable outskirts.
—Isn't there even a tree
    for the children? What sort of landlord

will we have? Too strict?
    in a necklace of coins, a porter
impervious as fate
    to the shudder in our pockets.

What kind of neighbour?
    Unmarried? Perhaps not noisy?
The old place was no pleasure
    but still the air there breathed

our atmosphere, was soaked
    in our own odours. Easy,
to put up with fetid air
    if it isn't soiled by outsiders!

It was old, of course, and
    rotting, but still ... Not a hostel room!
I don't know about being born
    but this is for dying in!

1922

41

Ophelia: in Defence of the Queen

Prince, let's have no more disturbing
    these wormy flower-beds. Look at
the living rose, and think of a woman
    snatching a single day—from the few left to her.

Prince Hamlet, you defile the Queen's
    womb. Enough. A virgin cannot
judge passion. Don't you know Phaedra
    was more guilty, yet men still sing of her,

and will go on singing. You, with your blend
    of chalk and rot, you bony
scandalmonger, how can you ever
    understand a fever in the blood?

Beware, if you continue . . . I can
    rise up through flagstones into the grand bed-chamber
of so much sweetness, I myself, to defend her.
    I myself—your own undying passion!

1923

Wherever you are I can reach you

Wherever you are I can reach you
to summon up—or send you back again!
Yet I'm no sorceress. My eyes grew sharp in
the white book—of that far-off river Don.

From the height of my cedar I see a world
where court decisions float, and all lights wander.
Yet from here I can turn the whole sea upside down
to bring you from its depths—or send you under!

You can't resist me, since I'm everywhere:
at daylight, underground, in breath and bread,
I'm always present. That is how I shall procure
your lips—as God will surely claim your soul—

in your last breath—and even in that choking hour
I'll be there, at the great Archangel's fence,
to put these bloodied lips up against the thorns
of Judgement—and to snatch you from your bier!

Give in! You must. This is no fairytale.
Give in! Any arrow will fall back on you.
Give in! Don't you know no one escapes
the power of creatures reaching out with

breath alone? (That's how I soar up
with my eyes shut and mica round my mouth . . .)
Careful, the prophetess tricked Samuel.
Perhaps I'll hoodwink you. Return alone,

because another girl is with you. Now on Judgement Day
there'll be no litigation. So till then
I'll go on wandering.
                           And yet I'll have your soul
as an alchemist knows how to win your

Lips . . .

1923

43

From WIRES

Along these singing lines that run
from pole to pole, supporting heaven,
I send along to you my portion
of earthly dust.
      From wires
to poles. This alley sighs
the telegraphic words: I lo-o-ve . . .

I beg. (No printed form would
hold that word! But wires are simpler.)
Atlas himself upon these poles
lowered the racetrack
of the Gods.
      Along these files
the telegraphic word: g-oo-oodbye . . .

Do you hear it? This last word
torn from my hoarse throat: Forg-i-ive . . .
Over these calm Atlantic fields
the rigging holds. And higher, higher,
all the messages fuse together
in Ariadne's web: Retu-u-rn . . .
And plaintive cries of: I won't leave . . .

These wires are steely guards upon
voices from Hell,

receding . . . far into that distance,
still implored for some compassion.

Compassion? (But in such a chorus
can you distinguish such a noise?)
That cry, arising as death comes—
through mounds—and ditches—that last
waft of her—passion that persists—
Euridice's: A-a-alas,

and not—a—

1923

7

Patiently, as tarmac under hammers,
patiently, as what is new matures,
patiently, as death must be awaited,
patiently, as vengeance may be nursed—

So I shall wait for you. (One look down to earth.
Cobblestones. Lips between teeth. And numb.)
Patiently, as sloth can be prolonged,
patiently, as someone threading beads.

Toboggans squeak outside; the door answers.
Now the wind's roar is inside the forest.
What has arrived is writing, whose corrections
are lofty as a change of reign, or a prince's entrance.

And let's go home!
this is inhuman—
Yet it's mine.

1923

Sahara

Young men, don't ride away! Sand
  stifled the soul of the
last one to disappear and now
  he's altogether dumb.

To look for him is useless.
  (Young men, I never lie.)
That lost one now reposes
  in a reliable grave.

He once rode into me as if
  through lands of
miracles and fire, with all
  the power of poetry, and

I was: dry, sandy, without day.
  He used poetry
to invade my depths, like those of
  any other country!

Listen to this story of two
  souls, without jealousy:
we entered one another's eyes
  as if they were oases—

I took him into me as if he were
  a god, in passion,
simply because of a charming tremor
  in his young throat.

Without a name he sank into me. But now
  he's gone. Don't search for him.
All deserts forget the thousands of
  those who sleep in them.

And afterwards the Sahara in one
   seething collapse will
cover you also with sand like sprinkled
   foam. And be your hill!

1923

The Poet

A poet's speech begins   a great way off.
A poet is   carried far away by speech

by way of planets, signs, and the   ruts
of roundabout parables, between *yes* and *no*,
in his hands even sweeping gestures from a bell-tower
become hook-like. For the way of comets

is the poet's way. And the blown-apart
links of causality   are his links. Look up
after him without hope. The eclipses of
poets are not foretold in the calendar.

He is the one that mixes up the cards
and confuses   arithmetic and weight,
demands answers from the school bench,
the one who altogether refutes Kant,

the one in the stone graves of the Bastille
who remains like a tree in its loveliness.
And yet the one whose   traces have always vanished,
the train everyone always arrives
too late to catch

for the path of comets
is the path of poets: they burn without warming,
pick without cultivating. They are: an explosion, a breaking in—
and the mane of their path makes the   curve of a
graph   cannot be foretold by the calendar.

There are superfluous people about in
this world, out of sight, who
aren't listed in any directory; and
home for them is   a rubbish heap.

They are hollow, jostled creatures:
who keep silent, dumb as dung, they are
nails   catching in your silken hem
dirt   imagined under your wheels.

Here they are, ghostly and invisible, the
sign is on them, like the speck of the leper.
People like Job in this world who
might even have envied him. If.

We are poets, which has the sound of outcast.
Nevertheless, we step out from our shores.
We dare contend for godhead, with goddesses,
and for the Virgin   with the gods themselves.

3

Now what shall I do here, blind and fatherless?
Everyone else can see and has a father.
Passion in this world has to leap anathema
as it might be over the walls of a trench
and weeping   is called a cold in the head.

What shall I do, by nature and trade
a singing creature (like a wire—sunburn! Siberia!)
as I go over the bridge of my enchanted
visions, that cannot be weighed, in a
world that deals only in weights and measures?

What shall I do, singer and first-born, in a
world where the deepest black is grey,
and inspiration is kept in   a thermos?
with all this immensity
in a measured world?

1923

Appointment

I'll be late for the meeting
we arranged. When I arrive, my hair
will be grey. Yes, I suppose I grabbed
at Spring. And you set your hopes much too high.

I shall walk with this bitterness for years
across mountains or town squares equally,
(Ophelia didn't flinch at rue!) I'll walk
on souls and on hands without shuddering.

Living on. As the earth continues.
With blood in every thicket, every creek.
Even though Ophelia's face is waiting
between the grasses bordering every stream.

She gulped at love, and filled her mouth
with silt. A shaft of light on metal!
I set my love upon you. Much too high.
In the sky   arrange my burial.

1923

Rails

The bed of a railway cutting
   has tidy sheets. The steel-blue
parallel tracks ruled out
   as neatly as staves of music.

And over them people are driven
   like possessed creatures from Pushkin
whose piteous song   has been silenced.
   Look, they're departing, deserting.

And yet lag behind and linger,
   the note of pain always rising
higher than love, as the poles freeze
   to the bank, like Lot's wife, forever.

Despair has appointed an hour for me
   (as someone arranges a marriage): then
Sappho with her voice gone
   I shall weep like a simple seamstress

with a cry of passive lament—
   a marsh heron! The moving train
will hoot its way over the sleepers
   and slice through them like scissors.

Colours blur in my eye,
   their glow a meaningless red.
All young women at times
   are tempted—by such a bed!

1923

You loved me

You loved me. And your lies had their own probity.
   There was a truth in every falsehood.
Your love went far beyond any possible
   boundary   as no one else's could.

Your love seemed to last even longer
   than time itself. Now you wave your hand—
and suddenly your   love for me is over!
   That is the truth in five words.

1923

It's not like waiting for post

It's not like waiting for post.
This is how you wait for
the one letter you need:
soft stuff bound with
tape and paste.
Inside a little word.
That's all. Happiness.

Waiting for happiness?
It's more like waiting for death.
The soldiers will salute
and three chunks of lead
will slam into your chest.
Your eyes will then flash red.

No question of joy.
Too old now, all bloom gone.
Waiting for what else now but
black muzzles in a square yard.

A square letter. I think
there may be spells in the ink.
No hope. And no one is
too old to face death

or such a square envelope.

1923

My ear attends to you

My ear attends to you,
as a mother hears in her sleep.
To a feverish child, she whispers
as I bend over you.

At the skin, my blood calls out to
your heart, my whole sky craves
an island of tenderness.
My rivers tilt towards you.

And I am drawn downwards
as stairs slope into a garden,
or some willow's bough falls
straight down, away from the milestone.

Stars are pulled to the earth
and laurels on graves won
with suffering, attract banners.
An owl longs for a hollow.

And I lean down
towards you with muscle and wing,
as if to a grave stone,
(I put the years to sleep)

my lips seek yours . . . like spring.

1923

As people listen intently

As people listen intently
   (a river's mouth to its source)
that's how they smell a flower
to the depths, till they lose all sense.

That's how they feel their deepest
   craving in dark air,
as children lying in blue sheets
peer into memory.

And that's how a young boy feels
when his blood begins to change.
   When people fall in love with love
they fling themselves in the abyss.

1923

Strong doesn't mate with strong

Strong doesn't mate with strong.
It's not allowed in this world.
So Siegfried missed Brunhilde,
in marriage fixed by a sword.

Like buffaloes, stone on stone,
in brotherly hatred joined,
he left their marriage bed, unknown,
she slept, unrecognized.

Apart, in the marriage bed.
Apart, in ambiguous language.
Apart, and clutched like a fist.
Too late.   And apart.   That's marriage.

More ancient evil yet:
Achilles, Thetis' son
crushing the Amazon
like a lion, missed Penthesilea.

Think of her glance, when felled
from her horse in the mud,
she looked up at him then
and not down from Olympus.

And afterwards, his passion was
to snatch his wife back from darkness?
But equal never mates with equal.

And so, we missed each other.

1924

In a world

In a world where most people
are hunched and sweaty
I know only one person
equal to me in strength.

In a world where there is
so much to want
I know only one person
equal to me in power.

In a world where mould
and ivy cover everything
I know only one person—you—
who equals me in spirit.

1924

POEM OF THE MOUNTAIN

Liebster, Dich wundert
die Rede? Alle Scheidenden
reden wie Trunkene und
nehmen sich festlich . . .
                    —Hölderlin

A shudder: off my shoulders
    with this mountain! My soul rises.
Now let me sing of sorrow which
    is my own mountain

a blackness which I will
    never block out again:
Let me sing of sorrow
    from the top of the mountain!

1

A mountain, like the body of
a recruit mown down by shells,
wanting lips that were
unkissed, and a wedding ceremony

the mountain demanded those.
Instead, an ocean broke into its ears
with sudden shouts of hooray! Though
the mountain fought and struggled.

The mountain was like thunder!
A chest drummed on by Titans.
(Do you remember that last house
of the mountain—the end of the suburb?)

The mountain was many worlds!
And God took a high price for one.
Sorrow began with a mountain.
This mountain looked on the town.

2

Not Parnassus   not Sinai
simply a bare and military
hill. Form up! Fire!
Why is it then in my eyes
(since it was October and not May)
that mountain was Paradise?

3

On an open hand Paradise was offered,
(if it's too hot, don't even touch it!)
threw itself under our feet with all
its gullies and steep crags,

with paws of Titans, with all
its shrubbery and pines
the mountain seized the skirts of our
coats, and commanded: stop.

How far from schoolbook Paradise
it was: so *windy*, when
the mountain pulled us down on our
backs. To itself. Saying: lie here!

The violence of that pull bewildered us.
How? Even now I don't know.
Mountain. Pimp. For holiness.
It pointed, to say: here.

How to forget Persephone's pomegranate
grain in the coldness of winter?
I remember lips half-opening to
mine, like the valves of a shell-creature

lost because of that grain, Persephone!
Continuous as the redness of lips,
and your eyelashes   were like jagged points
upon the golden angles of a star.

5

Not that passion is   deceitful or imaginary!
It doesn't lie. Simply, it doesn't last!
If only we could come into this world as though
we were common people in love

be sensible, see things as they are: this
is just a hill, just a bump in the ground.
(And yet they say it is by the pull of
abysses, that you measure height.)

In the heaps of gorse, coloured dim
among islands of tortured pines . . .
(In delirium above the level of
life)
        —Take me then. I'm yours.

Instead only the gentle mercies of
domesticity—chicks twittering—
because we came down into this world who
once lived at the height of heaven: in love.

6

The mountain was mourning (and mountains do mourn,
their clay is bitter, in the hours of parting).
The mountain mourned: for the tenderness
(like doves) of our undiscovered mornings.

The mountain mourned: for our friendliness, for
that unbreakable kinship of the lips.
The mountain declared that everyone will
receive in proportion to his tears.

The mountain grieved because   life is a gypsy-camp,
and we go marketing all our life from heart to heart.
And this was Hagar's grief. To be
sent far away. Even with her child.

Also the mountain said that all things were a trick
of some demon, no sense to the game.
The mountain sorrowed. And we were silent,
leaving the mountain to judge the case.

7

The mountain mourned for what is now blood
and heat will turn only to sadness.
The mountain mourned. It will not let us go.
It will not let you lie with someone else!

The mountain mourned, for what is now
world and Rome will turn   only to smoke.
The mountain mourned, because we shall be with
others. (And I do not envy them!)

The mountain mourned: for the terrible load
of promises, too late for us to renounce.
The mountain mourned the ancient nature of
the Gordian knot of law and passion.

The mountain mourned for our mourning also.
For tomorrow! Not yet! Above our foreheads
will break—death's sea of—memories!
For tomorrow, when we shall realize!

That sound   what?   as if someone were
crying just nearby? Can that be it?
The mountain is mourning. Because we must go down
separately, over such mud,

into life which we all know is nothing but
mob market barracks:
That sound said: all poems of
mountains   are written   *thus*

8

Hump of Atlas, groaning
   Titan, this town where we
live, day in, day out, will come
   to take a pride in the mountain

where we defeated life—at cards, and
   insisted with passion *not to*
exist. Like a bear-pit.
   And the twelve apostles.

Pay homage to my dark cave,
   (I was a cave that the waves entered).
The last hand of the card game was
   played, you remember, at the edge of the suburb?

Mountain   many worlds   the
   gods take revenge on their own likeness!

And my grief began with this mountain
which sits above me now like my headstone.

Years will pass. And then   the inscribed
slab will be changed for tombstone and removed.
There will be summerhouses on our mountain.
Soon it will be hemmed in with gardens,

because in outskirts like this they say
the air is better, and it's easier to live:
so it will be cut into plots of land,
and many lines of scaffolding will cross it.

They will straighten my mountain passes.
All my ravines will be upended.
There must be people who want to bring happiness
into their *home*, to have *happiness*.

Happiness at home! Love without fiction.
Imagine: without any stretching of sinews.
I have to be a woman   and endure this!
(There was happiness—when you used to come,

happiness—in my home.) Love without any extra
sweetness given by parting. Or a knife.
Now on the ruins of our happiness
a town will grow: of husbands and wives.

And in that same blessed air, while
you can, everyone   should sin—
soon shopkeepers on holidays
will be chewing the cud of their profits,

thinking out new levels and corridors, as
everything leads them back   to their house!
For there has to be someone who needs
a roof with a stork's nest!

Yet under the weight of these foundations
the mountain will not forget   the game.
Though people go astray   they must remember.
And the mountain has   mountains of time.

Obstinate crevices and cracks remain;
in summer homes, they'll realize, too late,
this is no hill, overgrown with families, but
a volcano! Make money out of that!

Can vineyards ever hold the danger
of Vesuvius? A giant without fear cannot
be bound with flax. And the delirium
of lips alone has   the same power:

to make the vineyards stir and turn heavily,
to belch out their lava of hate.
Your daughters shall all become prostitutes
and all your sons turn into   poets!

You shall rear a bastard child, my daughter!
Waste your flesh upon the gypsies, son!
May you never own a piece of fertile land
you   who take your substance from my blood.

Harder than any cornerstone, as
binding as the words of a dying man,
I curse you: do not look for happiness
upon my mountain   where you move like ants!

At some hour unforeseen, some time unknowable,
you will realize, the whole lot of you, how
enormous and without measure is
the mountain of God's seventh law.

Epilogue

There are blanks in memory   cataracts
on our eyes; the seven veils.
I no longer remember you separately
as a face but a white emptiness

without true features. All—is a
whiteness. (My spirit is one
uninterrupted wound.) The chalk of
details must   belong to tailors!

The dome of heaven was   built in a single frame
and oceans   are featureless   a mass of
drops that cannot be distinguished. You
are unique. And love is no detective.

Let now some neighbour say whether your
hair is black or fair, for he can tell.
I leave that to physicians or watchmakers.
What passion has a use for such details?

You are a full, unbroken circle, a
whirlwind or   wholly turned to stone.
I cannot think of you apart from
love. There is an   equals sign.

(In heaps of sleepy down, and falls of
water, hills of foam, there is
a new sound, strange to my hearing,
instead of I   a regal *we*)

and though life's beggared now and
narrowed into   how things are
still I cannot see you joined to
anyone: a
           revenge of memory.

finished 1 Dec 1924

POEM OF THE END

1

A single post, a point of rusting
  tin in the sky
marks the fated place we
  move to, he and I

on time   as death is
  prompt   strangely
too smooth the gesture of
  his hat to me

menace at the edges of his
  eyes   his mouth tight
shut   strangely too low is the
  bow he makes tonight

on time?   that false note in
  his voice, what
is it the brain alerts to and the
  heart drops at?

under that evil sky, that sign of
  tin and rust.
Six o'clock. There he is waiting
  by the post.

Now we kiss soundlessly, his
  lips stiff as
hands are given to queens, or
  dead people thus

round us the shoving elbows of
    ordinary bustle
and strangely irksome rises the
    screech of a whistle

howls like a dog screaming
    angrier, longer: what
a nightmare strangeness life is
    at death point

and that nightmare reached my waist
    only last night
and now reaches the stars, it has
    grown to its true height

crying silently love love until
    —Has it gone
six, shall we go to the cinema?
    I shout it: home!

2

And what have we come to?
    tents of nomads
thunder and drawn swords over
    our heads, some

terror we expect
    listen   houses
collapsing in the one
    word: home.

It is   the whine of a cossetted
    child lost, it is the
noise a baby makes for
    give and *mine*.

Brother in dissipation, cause
    of this cold fever, you
hurry now to get home just
    as men rush in leaving

like a horse jerking the
    line   rope down in the dust.
Is there even a building there?
    Ten steps before us.

A house on the hill   no higher   a
    house on the top of the hill and
a window under the roof   *is it*
    from the red sun alone

it is burning?   or is it my life
    which must begin again? how
simple poems are: it means I
    must go out into the night
                                    and talk to

who shall I tell my sorrow
    my horror greener than ice?
—You've been thinking too much.
    A solemn answer: yes.

3

And the embankment   I hold
   to water   thick and solid as
if we had come to the hanging
   gardens of Semiramis

to water   a strip as colourless
   as a slab for corpses
I am like a female singer holding
   to her music. To this wall.

Blindly   for you won't return
   or listen, even if I bend to
the quencher of all thirst, I am
hanging at the gutter of a roof.

Lunatic. It is not the river
   (I was born naiad) that makes me
shiver now, she was a hand I held
   to, when you walked beside me, a lover

and faithful.
                    The dead are faithful
though not to all in their cells; if
   death lies on my left now,
it is at your side I feel it.

Now a shaft of astonishing light, and
   laughter   that cheap tambourine.
—You and I must   have a talk. And
   I shiver: let's be brave, shall we?

A blonde mist, a wave of
gauze ruffles, of human
breathing, smoky exhalations
endless talk   the smell of
what? of haste and filth
connivance   shabby acts   all
the secrets of business men
   and ballroom powder.

Family men   like bachelors
move in their rings like middle-aged boys
always joking   always laughing, and
calculating, always calculating
large deals   and little ones, they are
snout-deep in the feathers of some
business arrangement
   and ballroom powder.

(I am half-turned away   is this
our house? I am not mistress here)
Someone   over his cheque book
another bends to a kid glove hand
a third works at a delicate foot
in patent leather   furtively   the smell
rises of marriage-broking
   and ballroom powder.

In the window is the silver
bite of a tooth: it is the Star of Malta,
which is the sign of stroking of the love
that leads to pawing and to pinching.
(Yesterday's food perhaps   but
nobody worries if it smells slightly)
   of dirt, commercial tricks
      and ballroom powder.

The chain is too short perhaps even
if it is not steel but platinum?
Look how their three chins shake
like cows munching their own veal
above their sugared necks
the devils swing on a gas lamp
   smelling of business slumps
and another powder
made by Berthold Schwartz
                             genius
intercessor for people:
—You and I must   have a talk
  —Let's be brave, shall we?

5

I catch a movement of his
  lips, but he won't
speak —You don't   love me?
  —Yes, but in torment

drained and driven to death
  (He looks round like an eagle)
—You call this   home? It's
  in the heart. —What *literature*!

For love is flesh, it is a
  flower flooded with blood.
Did you think it was just a
  little chat across a table

a snatched hour and back home again
  the way gentlemen and ladies
play at it? Either love is
—A shrine?
                   or else a scar.

A scar   every servant and guest
  can see (and I think silently:
love is a bow-string pulled
  back to the point of breaking).

Love is a bond. That has snapped for
  us   our mouths and lives part
(I begged you not to put a
  spell on me that holy hour

close on mountain heights of
  passion   memory is mist).
Yes, love is a matter of gifts
  thrown in the fire, for nothing

The shell-fish crack of his mouth
  is pale, no chance of a smile:
—Love is a large   bed.
  —Or else an empty gulf.

Now his fingers begin to
  beat, no mountains
move. Love is—
              —*Mine:* yes.
I understand. And so?

The drum beat of his fingers
  grows (scaffold and square)
—Let's go, he says. For me, let's
  die, would be easier.

Enough cheap stuff   rhymes
  like railway hotel rooms, so:
—love means life   although
  the ancients had a different

name.
   —Well?
                   A scrap
of handkerchief in a fist
like a fish. Shall we go? How,
   bullet   rail   poison

death anyway, choose: I make no
   plans. A Roman, you
survey the men still alive
   like an eagle:
                say goodbye.

6

I didn't want this, not
   this (but listen, quietly,
to want is what bodies do
   and now we are ghosts only).

And yet I   didn't say it
   though the time of the train is set
and the sorrowful honour of leaving
   is a cup given to women

or perhaps in madness I
   misheard you   polite liar:
is this the bouquet that you give your
   love, this blood-stained honour?

Is it? Sound follows
   sound clearly: was it goodbye
you said? (as sweetly casual
   as a handkerchief dropped without

thought) in this battle
    you are Caesar (What an
insolent thrust, to put the
    weapon of defeat, into my hand

like a trophy). It continues. To
    sound in my ears. As I bow.
—Do you always pretend
    to be forestalled in breaking?

Don't deny this, it
    is a vengeance of Lovelace
a gesture that does you credit
    while it lifts the flesh

from my bones. Laughter   the laugh of
    death. Moving. Without desire.
That is for others now
    we are shadows to one another.

Hammer the last nail in
    screw up the lead coffin.
—And now a last request.
    —Of course. Then say nothing

about us   to those who will
    come after me. (The sick
on their stretchers talk of spring.)
—May I ask the same thing?

—Perhaps I should give you a ring?
    —No. Your look is no longer open.
The stamp left on your heart
    would be the ring on your hand.

So now   without any scenes
       I must swallow, silently, furtively.
—A book then? No, you give those
       to everyone, don't even write them

       books . . .

So now   must   be no
so now   must   be no
must be no crying

In wandering tribes of
fishermen brothers
drink without crying

dance without crying
their blood is hot, they
pay without crying

pearls in a glass
melt, as they run their
world   without crying

                    Now I am going and this
                    Harlequin gives his
                    Pierrette a bone like
                    a piece of contempt

                    He throws her the honour
                    of ending the curtain, the last
                    word when one inch of lead in
                    the breast would be hotter and better

Cleaner. My   teeth
press my lips. I can
stop myself crying

pressing the sharpness
into the softest
so without crying

so tribes of nomads
die without crying
burn without crying.

So tribes of fishermen
in ash and song can
hide their dead man.

7

And the embankment. The last one.
    Finished. Separate, and hands apart
like neighbours avoiding one another. We
    walk away from the river, from my

cries. Falling salts of mercury
    I lick off without attention.
No great moon of Solomon
    has been set for my tears in the skies.

A post. Why not beat my forehead to
    blood on it? To smithereens! We are
like fellow criminals, fearing one
    another. (The murdered thing is love.)

Don't say these are lovers? Going into
    the night? Separately? To sleep with others?
You understand the future is up there?
    he says. And I throw back my head.

To sleep! Like newly-weds over their mat!
   To sleep! We can't fall into
step. And I plead miserably: take my
   arm, we aren't convicts to walk like this.

Shock! It's as though his *soul* has touched
   me   as his arm leans on mine. The electric
current beats along feverish wiring,
   and rips. He's leaned on my soul with his arm.

He holds me. Rainbows everywhere. What is more like a
   rainbow than tears? Rain, a curtain, denser
than beads. I don't know if such embankments can
   end. But here is a bridge and
                              —Well then?

Here? (The hearse is ready.)
   Peaceful   his eyes move
upward: couldn't you see me home?
   for the very last time.

8

Last   bridge   I won't
give up or take out my hand
this is the last bridge
the last bridging between

water   and firm land:
and I am saving these
coins for death
for Charon, the price of Lethe

this   shadow money
from my dark hand I press
soundlessly into
the shadowy darkness of his

78

shadow money it is
no gleam and tinkle in it
coins for shadows:
the dead have enough poppies

This bridge

Lovers for the most
part are without hope: passion
also is just
a bridge, a means of connection

It's warm: to nestle
close at your ribs, to move in
a visionary pause
towards nothing, beside nothing

no   arms no   legs
now, only the bone of my
side is alive where
it presses directly against you

life in that side
only, ear and echo is it: there
I stick like white to
egg yolk, or an eskimo to his fur

adhesive, pressing
joined to you: Siamese
twins are no nearer.
The woman you call mother

when she forgot
all things in motionless triumph
only to carry you:
she did not hold you closer.

Understand: we have
grown into one as we slept and
now I can't jump
because I can't let go your hand

and I won't be torn off
as I press close to you: this
bridge is no husband
but a lover: a just slipping past

our support: for the
river is fed with bodies!
I bite in like a tick
you must tear out my roots to be rid of me

like ivy   like a tick
inhuman   godless
to throw me away like a thing,
when there is

no thing I ever prized
in this empty world of things.
Say this is only dream,
night still and afterwards morning

an express   to Rome?
Granada? I won't know myself
as I push off
the Himalayas of bedclothes.

But this dark is deep:
now I warm you with my blood, listen
to this flesh.
It is far truer than poems.

If you are warm, who
will you go to tomorrow for that?
This is delirium,
please say this bridge cannot

end
        as it ends.

—Here then? His gesture could
be made by a child, or a god.
—And so? —I am biting in!
For a little more time. The last of it.

9

Blatant as factory buildings,
    as alert to a call
here is the sacred and sublingual
    secret wives keep from husbands and

widows from friends, here is the full
    story that Eve took from the tree:
I am no more than an animal that
    someone has stabbed in the stomach.

Burning. As if the soul had been
    torn away with the skin. Vanished like steam
through a hole is that well-known foolish
    heresy called a soul.

That Christian leprosy:
    steam: save that with your poultices.
There never was such a thing.
    There was a body once, wanted to

live   no longer wants to live.

81

Forgive me! I didn't mean it!
　　The shriek of torn entrails.
So prisoners sentenced to death wait
　　for the 4 a.m. firing squad.

At chess perhaps with a grin
　　they mock the corridor's eye.
Pawns in the game of chess:
　　someone is playing with us.

Who? Kind gods or? Thieves?
　　The peephole is filled with an
eye　　　and the red corridor
　　clanks. Listen　　　the latch lifts.

One drag on tobacco, then
　　spit, it's all over, spit,
along this paving of chess squares
　　is a direct path　　　to the ditch

to blood. And the secret eye
　　the dormer eye of the moon.

And now, squinting sideways, how
　　far away you are already.

10

Closely, like one creature, we
start: there is our café!

There is our island, our shrine, where
in the morning, we people of the

rabble, a couple for a minute only,
conducted a morning service:

with things from country markets, sour
things seen through sleep or   spring.
The coffee was nasty there
entirely made from oats (and

with oats you can extinguish
caprice in fine race-horses).
There was no smell of Araby.
Arcadia was in

that coffee.

But how *she* smiled at us
and sat us down by her,
sad and worldly in her wisdom
a grey-haired paramour.

Her smile was solicitous
(saying: you'll wither! live!),
it was a smile at madness and being
penniless, at yawns   and love

and—this was the chief thing—
at laughter   without reason
smiles   with no deliberation
and our faces   without wrinkles.

Most of all   at youth
at passions   out of this climate
blown in from some other place
flowing from some other source

into that dim café
(burnous and Tunis) where
she smiled at hope and flesh
under old-fashioned clothes.

(My dear friend   I don't complain.
It's just another scar.)
To think how she saw us off,
that proprietress in her cap

stiff   as a Dutch hat . . .

Not quite remembering, not quite
understanding, we are led away from the festival—
along our street!   no longer ours   that
we walked many times, and no more shall.

Tomorrow the sun will rise in the West.
And then David will break with Jehovah.
—What are we doing?—We are *separating*.
—That's a word that means nothing to me.

It's the most inhumanly senseless
of words: *sep   arating*. (Am I one of a hundred?)
It is simply a word of four syllables and
behind their sound lies: emptiness.

Wait! Is it even correct in Serbian or
Croatian? Is it a Czech whim, this word.
Sep   aration! To *sep   arate!*
It is insane   unnatural

a sound to burst the eardrums, and spread out
far beyond the limits of longing itself.
Separation—the word is not in the Russian
language. Or the language of women. Or men.

Nor in the language of God. What are we—sheep?
To stare about us as we eat.
Separation—in what language is it,
when the meaning itself doesn't exist?

or even the sound! Well—an empty one, like
the noise of a saw in your sleep perhaps.
Separation. That belongs to the school of
Khlebnikov's   nightingale-groaning

swan-like . . .
                so how does it happen?
Like a lake of water running dry.
Into air. I can feel our hands touching.
To separate. Is a shock of thunder

upon my head—oceans rushing into
a wooden house. This is Oceania's
furthest promontory. And the streets are steep.
To separate. That means to go downward

downhill   the sighing sound of two
heavy soles   and at last a hand receives
the nail in it. A logic that turns
everything over. *To separate*

means we have to become
single creatures   again

we who had grown into one.

12

Dense as a horse mane is:
    rain in our eyes. And hills.
We have passed the suburb.
    Now we are out of town,

which is there   but not for us.
    Stepmother   not mother.
Nowhere   is lying ahead.
    And here   is where we fall.

85

A field with. A fence and.
   Brother and sister. Standing.
Life is   only a suburb:
   so you must build elsewhere.

Ugh, what a lost cause
   it is, ladies and gentlemen,
for the whole world is   suburb:
   Where   are the real towns?

Rain rips at us madly.
   We stand and break with each other.
In three months, these must be
   the first moments of sharing.

Is it true, God, that you even
   tried to borrow from Job?
Well, it didn't come off.
   Still. We are. Outside town.

Beyond it! Understand? Outside!
   That means   we've passed the walls.
Life is a place where it's forbidden
   to live. Like the Hebrew quarter.

And isn't it more worthy to
   become an eternal Jew?
Anyone not   a reptile
   suffers the same pogrom.

Life is for converts only
   Judases of all faiths.
Let's go to leprous islands
   or hell   anywhere   only not

life   which puts up with traitors, with
    those who are sheep   to butchers!
This paper which gives me the
    right to live—I stamp. With my feet.

Stamp! for the shield of David.
    Vengeance! for heaps of bodies
and they say after all (delicious) the
    Jews didn't want to live!

Ghetto of the chosen. Beyond this
    ditch. No mercy
In this   most Christian of worlds
    all poets   are Jews.

13

This is how they sharpen knives on a
    stone, and sweep sawdust up with
brooms. Under my hands there is
    something wet and furry.

Now where are those twin male
    virtues: strength, dryness?
Here beneath my hand I can
    feel   tears. Not rain!

What temptations can still be
    spoken of? Property is   water.
Since I felt your diamond eyes under
    my hands, flowing.

There is no more I can lose. We have
    reached the end of ending.
And so I simply stroke, and
    stroke. And stroke your face.

This is the kind of pride we have:
   Marinkas   are Polish girls.
Since now the eyes of an eagle weep
   underneath these hands . . .

Can you be crying? My friend, my
   —everything! Please forgive me!
How large and salty now is the
   taste of that in my fist.

Male tears are—cruel! They
   rise over my head! Weep,
there will soon be others to
   heal any guilt towards me.

Fish of   identic-
   al sea. A sweep upward! like
. . . any dead shells and any
   lips upon lips.

In tears.
Wormwood
to taste.
—And tomorrow
when
I am awake?

14

   A slope like a path   for
   sheep. With town noises.
   Three trollops approaching.
   They are laughing. At tears.

They are laughing   the full noon of
their bellies shake, like waves!
They laugh at the
                            inappropriate
disgraceful, male

tears of yours, visible
through the rain   like scars!
Like a shameful   pearl on
the bronze of a warrior.

These first and last tears
pour them now—for me—
for your tears   are pearls
that I wear in my crown.

And my eyes are not lowered.
I stare through   the shower.
Yes, dolls of Venus
stare at me! because

This is a closer bond
than the transport of lying down.
The Song of Songs itself
gives place to our speech,

infamous birds as we are
Solomon bows to us, for
our simultaneous cries
are   something more than a dream!

And into the hollow waves of
darkness—hunched and level—
without trace—in silence—
something sinks like a ship.

1924

An Attempt at Jealousy

How is your life with the other one,
    simpler, isn't it? One   stroke of the oar
then a long coastline, and soon
    even the memory of me

will be a floating island
    (in the sky, not on the waters):
spirits, spirits, you will be
    sisters, and never lovers.

How is your life with an ordinary
    woman?   without godhead?
Now that your sovereign has
    been deposed (and you have stepped down).

How is your life? Are you fussing?
    flinching? How   do you get up?
The tax of deathless vulgarity
    can you cope with it, poor man?

'Scenes and hysterics   I've had
    enough! I'll rent my own house.'
How is your life with the other one
    now, you that I chose for my own?

More to your taste, more delicious
    is it, your food? Don't moan if you sicken.
How is your life with an *image*
    you, who walked on Sinai?

How is your life with a stranger
    from this world? Can you (be frank)
love her? Or do you   feel shame
    like Zeus' reins on your forehead?

How is your life? Are you
    healthy? How do you   sing?
How do you deal with the pain
    of an undying conscience, poor man?

How is your life with a piece of market
    stuff, at a steep price.
After Carrara marble,
    how is your life with the dust of

plaster now? (God was hewn from
    stone, but he is smashed to bits.)
How do you live with one of a
    thousand women   after Lilith?

Sated with newness, are you?
    Now you are grown cold to magic,
how is your life with an
    earthly woman, without a sixth

sense? Tell me: are you happy?
    Not? In a shallow pit How is
your life, my love? Is it as
    hard as mine with another man?

                                        1924

To Boris Pasternak

Distance: versts, miles . . .
divide us; they've dispersed us,
to make us behave quietly
at our different ends of the earth.

Distance: how many miles of it
lie between us now—disconnected—
crucified—then dissected.
And they don't know—it unites us.

Our spirits and sinews fuse,
there's no discord between us.
though our separated pieces
                              lie outside
the moat—for eagles!

This conspiracy of miles
has not yet disconcerted us,
however much they've pushed us, like
orphans into backwaters.

—What then? Well. Now it's March!
And we're scattered like some pack of cards!

1925

From THE RATCATCHER

From Chapter 1

Hamelin, the good-mannered
  town of window-boxes,
well-stocked with
  warehouses
         Paradise Town!

How God must love
  these sensible
townspeople. Every one
  is righteous:

Goody-goody, always-right, always-provided-for,
stocked-up-in-time. It's Paradise Town!

Here are no riddles.
  All is smooth and peaceable.
Only good habits in
        Paradise
        Town.

In God's sweet
  backwater
(The Devil turns his
  nose up here):

It's goody-goody Paradise (owned by Schmidt and Mayers).
A town for an Emperor. Give way to your elders!

Everywhere is tranquil.
  No fire. The whole place
must belong to Abel.
  Isn't that
        Paradise?

Those who are not
  too cold or too hot
travel straight to Hamelin
  straight into Hamelin:

Lullaby and ermine-down, this is Paradise Town!
Everywhere is good advice and go-to-sleep on time Town!
First watch!
First watch!
With the world all contact's lost!
Is the dog out? And the cat in?
Did you hear the early warning.

Take your servants out of harness
  Shake your pipe—you've time for that—
but leave your workbench now because
  '*Morgen ist auch ein tag*'

Ten to ten!
Ten to ten.
Put your woolly earplugs in.
In the desk with all your schoolbooks
Set your clocks to ring at five.

Shopkeeper, leave your chalk,
  Housewife, your mending.
Look to your feather bed:
  '*Morgen ist auch ein tag*'

Ten o'clock.
Ten o'clock
No more interruptions.
Keys turned? Bolts drawn?
That was the third call.

Cl-o-ose your Bible, Dad.
Housewife, put your bonnet on.
Hus-band, your nightcap.
'*Morgen ist* . . .'

All asleep.
That's the Hameliners!

From Chapter 2

Dreams

In all other cities,
   in mine, for instance, (out of bounds)
husbands see mermaids, and
   wives dream of Byrons.

Children see devils,
   and servants see horsemen.
But what can these, Morpheus,
   citizens so sinless

dream of at night—Say *what*?
   They don't need to think hard.
The husband sees—his wife!
   The wife sees her husband!

The baby sees a teat.
   And that beauty, fat of cheek,
sees a sock of her father's
   that she's been darning.

The Cook tries the food out.
   The 'Ober' gives his orders.
It's all as it ought to be,
   all as it ought to be.

As stitches go smoothly
    along a knitting needle
Peter sees Paul (what else?).
    And Paul sees Peter.

A grandfather dreams of
    grandchildren.
Journalists—of some full-stop!
    The maid—a kind master.

Commandments for Kaspar.
    A sermon for the Pastor.
To sleep has its uses,
    it isn't really wasteful!

The sausage-maker dreams of
    poods of fat sausages;
a judge of a pair of scales
    (like the apothecary).

Teachers dream of canes.
    A tailor of goods for sale.
And a dog of his bone?
    Wrong! He sees his collar!

The Cook sees a plucked bird.
    The laundress sees velveteen.
Just as it's been laid down
    in the prescription.

And what of the Burgomeister?
    Sleep is like waking
once you are Burgomeister
    what else can you dream about?

Except looking over
   the citizens who serve you.
That's what the Burgomeister
   sees: all his servants!

That's how things have to be!
   That's how they are arranged!
That's the prescription!
   That's the prescription!

(My tone may be playful—yes,
   the old has some virtue)
So let us not use up
   our rhymes over nothing.

As the Burgomeister sleeps, let's
   slip into his room (Tsar
of Works and Constructions!)
   How solidly the building stands . . .

It's worth our attention.

From *The Children's Paradise*

To live means—ageing,
turning grey relentlessly.
To live is—for those you hate!
Life has no eternal things.

In my kingdom: no butchers, no jails.
   Only ice there! Only blue there!
Under the roof of shivering waters
   pearls the size of walnuts

girls wear and boys hunt.
There's—a bath—for everyone.

Pearls are a wondrous illness.
Fall asleep then. Sleep. And vanish.

Dry twigs are grey. Do you want
scarlet?—Try my coral branch!

In my kingdom: no mumps; no measles,
    medieval history, serious matters,
no execution of Jan Hus. No discrimination.
    No more need for childish terrors.

Only blue. And lovely Summer.
Time—for all things—without measure.

Softly, softly, children. You're
going to a quiet school—under the water.

Run with your rosy cheeks
into the eternal streams.

Someone: Chalk. Someone: Slime.
Someone calling: Got my feet wet.

Someone: Surge. Someone: Rumble.
Someone: Got a gulp of lake!

2

Diving boys and swimming girls
Look, the water's on their fingers.

Pearls are scattered for them!
The water's at their ankles,

sneaking up their little knees. They cry:
—Chrys—o—lite.

Red moss! Blue caves!
(Feet go deeper. Skies rise higher.)

Mirror boxes. Crystal halls. Something's
been left behind, something grows closer . . .

You're stuck up to the knees! Careful.
—Ah this chrys-o-prase!

The water is shoulder high on
little mice in schoolday clothes.

Little snub-nose,—higher, higher
now the water's at your throat.

It's sweeter than bed linen . . .
—Crystals! Crystals!

In my kingdom: (The flute sounds the gentlest *dolce*)
    Time dwindles, eyes grow larger.
Is that a sea gull? or is it a baby's bonnet?
    Legs grow heavy, hearts grow lighter.

Water reaches to the chin.
Mourn, friends and relatives!

Isn't this a fine palace
for the burgomeister's daughter?

Here are eternal dreams, woods without pathways.
    The flute grows sweeter, hearts more quiet.
Follow without thinking. Listen. No need for thought!
    The flute becomes sweeter still, hearts even quieter.

—*Mutter*. Don't call me in for supper . . .
                                    Bu-u-bbles!

                                            1925

From POEMS TO A SON

Forget us, children. Our conscience
   need not belong to you.
You can be free to write the tale
   of your own days and passions.

Here in this family album
   lies the salt family of Lot.
It is for you to reckon up
   the many claims on Sodom.

You didn't fight your brothers
   my curly headed boy!
So this is your time, this is your day.
   The land is purely yours.

Sin, cross, quarrel, anger,
   these are ours. There have been
too many funerals held by now
   for an Eden you've never seen

whose fruit you never tasted.
   So now, put off your mourning.
Understand: they are blind
   who lead you, but then

our quarrel is not your quarrel,
   So as you rush from Meudon
and race to the Kuban
   children, prepare for battle

in the field of your own days.

                January 1932

Homesickness

Homesickness! that long
exposed weariness!
It's all the same to me now
where I am   altogether lonely

or what stones I wander over
home with a shopping bag to
a house that is no more mine
than a hospital or a barracks.

It's all the same to me, captive
lion   what faces I move through
bristling, or what human crowd will
cast me out   as it must

into myself, into my separate internal
world, a Kamchatka bear without ice.
Where I fail to fit in (and I'm not trying) or
where I'm humiliated   it's all the same.

And I won't be seduced by the thought of
my native language, its milky call.
How can it matter   in what tongue I
am misunderstood by whoever I meet

(or by what readers, swallowing
newsprint, squeezing for gossip?)
They all belong to the twentieth
century, and   I am before time,

stunned, like a log left
behind from an avenue of trees.
People are all the same to me, everything
is the same, and it may be the most

indifferent of all   are these
signs and tokens which once were
native   but the dates have been
rubbed out: the soul was born somewhere.

For my country has taken so little care
of me that even the sharpest spy could
go over my whole spirit and would
detect no native stain there.

Houses are alien, churches are empty
everything   is the same:
But if by the side of the path one
particular bush rises
                    the rowanberry . . .

                                        1934

I opened my veins

I opened my veins.   Unstoppably
life spurts out with no remedy.
Now I set out bowls and plates.
Every bowl will be shallow.
Every plate will be small.
          And overflowing their rims,
into the black earth, to nourish
the rushes unstoppably
without cure, gushes
poetry . . .

1934

Epitaph

1

Just going out for a minute—
left your work (which the idle
call chaos) behind on the table.
And left the chair behind when   you went where?

I ask around all Paris, for it's
only in stories or pictures
that people rise to the skies:
where is your soul gone, where?

In the cupboard, two-doored like a shrine,
look   all your books are in place.
In each line the letters are there.
Where has it gone to, your face?

Your face
your warmth
your shoulder

where did they go?

2

Useless with eyes   like nails to
penetrate the black soil.
As true   as a nail in the mind
you are not here, not here.

It's useless   turning my eyes
and fumbling round the whole sky.
Rain. Pails of rain-water. But
you are not there, not there.

Neither one of the two. Bone is
too much bone. And spirit is too much spirit.
Where is the real you? All of you?
Too much here. Too much there.

And I won't exchange you for sand
and steam. You took me for kin,
and I won't give you up for a corpse
and a ghost: a here, and a there.

It's not you, not you, not you,
however much priests intone
that death and life are one:
God's too much God, worm—too much worm!

You are one thing, corpse and spirit.
We won't give you up for the smoke of
censers
or flowers
on graves

If you *are* anywhere, it's here in
us: and we honour best all those who
have gone by despising division.
It is all of you   that has gone.

3

Because once when you were young and bold
you did not leave me to rot alive among
bodies without souls or fall dead among walls
I will not let you   die altogether.

Because, fresh and clean, you took me
out by the hand, to freedom   and brought spring leaves
in bundles into my house   I shall not
let you be grown over with weeds and forgotten.

And because you met the status of my
first grey hairs like a son   with pride
greeting their terror with a child's joy:
I shall not let you go grey into men's hearts.

4

The blow   muffled through years of
   forgetting, of not knowing:
That blow reaches me now like the song of a
   woman, or like horses neighing.

Through an inert building, a song of passion and
   the blow comes:
dulled by forgetfulness, by not knowing which is
   a soundless thicket.

It is the sin of memory, which has no eyes or
   lips or flesh or nose,
the silt of all the days and nights
   we have been without each other

the blow is muffled with moss and waterweed:
   so ivy devours the
core of the living thing it is ruining
   —a knife through a feather bed.

Window wadding, our ears are plugged with it
   and with that other wool
outside windows of snow and the weight of spiritless
   years: and the blow is muffled.

1935

Readers of Newspapers

It crawls, the underground snake,
crawls, with its load of people.
And each one   has his
newspaper, his skin
disease; a twitch of chewing;
newspaper *caries*.
Masticators of gum,
readers of newspapers.

And who are the readers? old men? athletes?
soldiers? No face, no features,
no age. Skeletons—there's no
face, only the newspaper page.

All Paris   is dressed
this way from forehead to navel.
Give it up, girl, or
you'll give birth to
a reader of newspapers.

Sway   he lived with his sister.
Swaying   he killed his father.
They blow themselves up with pettiness
as if they were swaying with drink.

For such gentlemen   what
is the sunset or the sunrise?
They swallow emptiness,
these readers of newspapers.

For news   read: calumnies.
For news   read: embezzling,
in every column   slander
every paragraph some   disgusting thing.

With what, at the Last Judgement
will you come before the light?
Grabbers of small moments,
readers of newspapers.

Gone! lost! vanished! so,
the old maternal terror.
But mother, the Gutenberg Press
is more terrible than Schwarz' powder.

It's better to go to a graveyard
than into the   prurient
sickbay of scab-scratchers,
these readers of newspapers.

And who is it rots our sons
now in the prime of their life?
Those corrupters of blood
the *writers* of newspapers.

Look, friends   much
stronger than in these lines, do
I think this, when with
a manuscript in my hand

I stand before the face
there is no   emptier place
than before the absent
face of an editor of news-
                         papers' evil filth.

1935

Desk

1

My desk, most loyal friend
　　thank you. You've been with me on
every road I've taken.
　　My scar and my protection.

My loaded writing mule.
　　Your tough legs have endured
the weight of all my dreams, and
　　burdens of piled-up thoughts.

Thank you　　　for toughening me.
　　No worldly joy could pass
your severe looking-glass
　　you blocked the first temptation,

and every base desire
　　your heavy oak outweighed
lions of hate, elephants
　　of spite　　　you intercepted.

Thank you for growing with me
　　as my need grew in size
I've been laid out across you
　　so many years　　　alive

while you've grown broad and wide
　　and overcome me.　　　Yes,
however my mouth opens
　　you stretch out　　　limitless.

You've nailed me to your wood.
   I'm glad.   To be pursued.
And torn up.   At first light.
   To be caught.   And commanded:

Fugitive. Back to your chair!
   I'm glad you've guarded me
and bent my life away
   from blessings that don't last,

as wizards guide sleep walkers!
   My battles burn as signs.
You even use my blood to set out
   all my acts in lines—

in columns, as you are a pillar
   of light. My source of power!
You lead me as the Hebrews once
   were led forward by fire.

Take blessings now from me,
   as one put to the test, on
elbows, forehead, knotted knees,
   your knife edge   to my breast.

2

I celebrate thirty years
   of union   truer than love
I know every notch in your wood.
You know the lines in my face.

Haven't you written them there?
   devouring reams of paper
denying me any tomorrow
   teaching me only today.

You've thrown my important letters
   and money   in floods together,
repeating: for every single verse
   today has to be the deadline.

You've warned me of retribution
   not to be measured in spoonfulls.
And when   my body will be laid out,
   great fool! Let it be on you then.

3

The rest of you can eat me up
   I just record your behaviour!
For you they'll find dining tables
   to lay you out   This desk for me!

Because I've been happy with little
   there are foods I've never tasted.
The rest of you dine slowly.
   You've eaten too much and too often.

Places are already chosen
   long before birth for everyone.
The place of adventure is settled,
   and the places of gratification.

Truffles for you not pencils.
   Pickles instead of dactyls
and you express your pleasure
   in belches and not in verses.

At your head funeral candles
   must be thick-legged asparagus:
surely your road from this world
   will cross a dessert table!

111

Let's puff Havana tobacco
   on either side of you then;
and let your shrouds be made
   from the finest of Dutch linen.

And so as not to waste such
   fine cloth let them shake you
with left-overs and crumbs
   into the grave that waits for you.

Your souls at the   post mortem
   will be like stuffed capons.
But I shall be there naked
   with only two wings for cover.

                                        1933–5

Bus

The bus jumped, like a brazen
evil spirit,   a demon
cutting across the traffic
in streets as cramped as footnotes,
it rushed on its way   shaking
like a concert-hall vibrating
with applause.   And we shook in it!
Demons too.   Have you seen
seeds under a tap? We were
like peas in boiling soup,
or Easter toys dancing in
alcohol.   Mortared grain!
Teeth in a chilled mouth.

What   has been shaken out   someone
could use for a chandelier:
all the beads   and the bones
of an old woman. A necklace
on that girl's breast. Bouncing.
The child at his mother's nipple.
Shaken without reference
like pears   all of us   shaken
in *vibrato*, like violins.
The violence shook our souls
into laughter, and back into childhood.

Young again. Yes. The joy of that
being thrown into girlhood! Or
perhaps further back, to become
a tomboy with toothy grin.
       It was as if the piper
       had lead us, not out of town, but
       right out of the calendar.

Laughter exhausted us all.
I was too weak to stand.
Enfeebled, I kept on my feet only
by holding your belt in my hand.

Askew, head on, the bus was
crazed like a bull, it leapt
as if at a red cloth,
to rush round a sharp bend
and then, quite suddenly
stopped.
            . . . So, between hills, the creature
            lay obedient and still.
            Lord, what blue surrounded us,
            how everywhere was green!

The hurt of living gone,
like January's tin.
Green was everywhere,
a strange and tender green.

A moist, uneasy noise of green
flowed through our veins' gutters.
Green struck my head open,
and freed me from all thinking!

A moist, wood-twig smoke of green
flowed through our veins' gutters.
Green struck my head open.
It overflowed me completely!

Inside me, warmth and birdsong.
You could drink both of them from
the two halves of my skull—
(Slavs did that with enemies).

Green rose, green shoots, green
fused to a single emerald.
The green smell of the earth had
struck deeply. (No buffalo feels that.)

Malachite. Sapphire. Unneeded.
The eye and ear restored—
Falcons don't see tillage,
prisoners don't hear birds.

My eye is ripe with green.
Now I see no misfortune
(or madness—it was true reason!)
to leave a throne and fall

on all fours like a beast
and dig his nose in the grass . . .
He wasn't mad, that sovereign
Nebuchadnezzar, munching

stalks of grass—but a Tsar,
an herbivorous, cereal-loving
brother of Jean-Jacques Rousseau . . .
This green of the earth has given
my legs the power to run

into heaven.
I've taken in so much
green juice and energy I am
as powerful as a hero.
The green of the earth has struck
my cheeks. And there it glows.

For an hour, under cherry trees,
God allowed me to think
that my own, my old, face
could be the same colour as these.

Young people may laugh. Perhaps
I'd be better off standing under
some old tower, than mistaking
that cherry-tree colour
for the colour of my

face . . .

With grey hair like mine? But then,
apple blossom is grey. And God has brought me close
to everyone of his creatures
I am *closer*   as well as *lower* . . .

a sister to all creation
from the buttercup to the mare—
So I blew in my hands, like a trumpet.
I even dared to leap!

As old people rejoice
without shame on a roundabout,
I believed my hair was brown
again, no grey streak in it.

So, with my branch of green
I could drive my friend like a goose,
and watch his sail-cloth suit
turn into true sails—

Surely my soul was prepared
to sail beyond the ocean.
(The earth had been a seabed—
it laughed now with vegetation.)

My companion was only slender
    in the waist.   His heart was thick.
(How his white canvas puckered,
    and came to rest in the green.)

Faith. Aurora. Soul's blue.
   Never dilute or measured.
Idiot soul!   And yet Peru
   will yield to the madness of it!

My friend became heavy to lead,
   as a child does for no reason,
(I found my own bold web
   as lovely as any spider's)

Suddenly   like a vast frame
for a living miracle: Gates!
Between their marble, I could
stand, like an ancient sign,

uniting myself and the landscape;
a frame in which I remain,
between gates that lead to no castle,
gates that lead to no farmhouse,

gates   like a lion's jaws
which let in light. Gates
leading to where? Into
happiness   came the answer,

twofold . . .

Happiness? Far away.   North of here.
Somewhere else. Some other time.
Happiness? Even the scent is cold.
I looked for it once, on all fours.

When I was four years old, looking
for a clover with four leaves.
What do these numbers matter?
Happiness? Cows feed on it.

The young are in ruminant company
of two jaws and four hooves.
Happiness stamps its feet.
It doesn't stand looking at gates.

The wood block and the well.
Remember that old tale?
Of cold water streaming past
an open, longing mouth,

and the water missing the mouth
as if in a strange dream.
There's never enough water,
(the sea's not enough for me).

From opened veins, water
flows on to moist earth—
Water keeps passing by
as life does, in a dream.

And now I've wiped my cheeks
I know the exact force
of the streams that miss my hands
and pass my thirsting

mouth

The tree, in its cloud of blossom,
was a dream avalanche over us.
With a smile, my companion compared it
to a 'cauliflower in white sauce'.

That phrase struck into my heart, loud
as thunder. Now grant me encounters
with thieves and pillagers, Lord, rather
than bed in the hay with a *gourmand*!

A thief can rob—and not touch your face.
You'll be fleeced, but your soul will escape.
But a *gourmand* must finger and pinch, before
he puts you aside, to eat later.

I can throw off my rings. Or my fingers.
You can strip my hide, and wear it.
But a *gourmand* demands the brain and heart
to the last groan of their torment.

The thief will go off. In his pockets
my jewels, the cross from my breast.
A toothbrush ends all romance
with *gourmands*.

                    Don't fall in their hands!

And you, who could be loved royally
as an evergreen, shall be
as nameless as cauliflower in my mouth:
I take this revenge—for the tree!

                    1934–6

When I look at the flight of the leaves

When I look at the flight of the leaves in
　　their floating down on to the paving of cobbles
and see them swept up as if by an
　　artist who has finished his picture at last

I think how (already nobody likes either
　　the way I stand, or my thoughtful face)
a manifestly yellow, decidedly
　　rusty leaf—has been left behind on the tree.

1936

From POEMS TO CZECHOSLOVAKIA

6

They took   quickly, they took   hugely,
  took the mountains and their entrails.
They took our coal, and took our steel
  from us, lead they took also and crystal.

They took the sugar, and they took the clover
  they took the North and took the West.
They took the hive, and took the haystack
  they took the South from us, and took the East.

Vary   they took and Tatras   they took,
  they took the near at hand and far away.
But   worse than taking paradise on earth from us
  they won the battle for our native land.

Bullets they took from us, they took our rifles
  minerals they took, and comrades too.
But while our mouths have spittle in them
  the whole country   is still armed.

8

What tears in eyes now
weeping with anger and love
Czechoslovakia's tears
Spain in its own blood

and what a black mountain
has blocked the world   from the light.
It's time—It's time—It's time
to give back to God   his ticket.

I refuse to be. In
the madhouse of the inhuman
I refuse   to live.
With the wolves of the market place

I refuse   to howl.
Among the sharks of the plain
I refuse to swim   down
where moving backs make a current.

I have no need of holes
for ears, nor prophetic eyes:
to your mad world there is
one answer: to refuse!

1938

Note to 1971 edition: on Working Method

No poet's voice can be exactly recorded in the medium of another language. Marina Tsvetaeva's is particularly difficult to capture, both because her consistent adherence to rhyme and to metrical regularity would, if copied in the English poems, probably enfeeble them, and because so many of the linguistic devices which she powerfully exploits (such as ellipsis, changes of word-order, the throwing into relief of inflectional endings) are simply not available in English. On the whole, the English versions are consciously less emphatic, less loudly-spoken, less violent, often less jolting and disturbing than the Russian originals. Most noticeable of all in Tsvetaeva's poems, especially the later ones, are the very strong rhythm and the unprecedentedly vigorous syntax. There is, too, a somewhat idiosyncratic and highly emotional use of punctuation, particularly of exclamation marks and dashes.

Except in the case of 'Poem of the Mountain', a literal version of which was prepared by Valentina Coe, and a number of earlier poems, where the literal version was dictated on to a tape-recorder, Elaine Feinstein and I worked as follows: I would write out each poem in English, keeping as close as made sense to the word-order of the Russian; joining by hyphens those English words which represented a single Russian word; indicating by oblique lines words whose order had to be reversed to be readable, and by asterisks phrases where several changes had had to take place; adding notes on metre, sound properties, play with word-roots, and specifically Russian connotations. All this *material* was then changed into poetry by Elaine Feinstein, who took those liberties with it that the new English poem demanded, but returned constantly to the Russian text to check the look, sound, and position of Tsvetaeva's own words.

To give one example—the opening of lyric 6 of 'Poem of the End'. One of the most original and effective features of the poems making up this cycle is the way they tend to be structurally based each upon a single syntactic unit which is several times repeated almost identically. This determines the structure of every stanza in which it appears, throwing into different kinds of relief the words and phrases that are not part of it, and bringing a peculiar rhythm into the expressed emotion. When it ceases to recur, we read the rest of the poem in strong recollection of its shape.

In lyric 6 the dominant phrase (*italicized*, by me, in the extract below) is one that has the verb 'to hand' as its final and basic element, and involves the prominent use of the dative case. Each time, the phrase is in brackets and, each time, its last word comes as an enjambment. It occurs in stanzas 2, 3 and 5; is implied in stanza 4; and is referred to (through similar enjambment and rhythm) in stanza 6, where a sharp irony arises from the combination of the rhythm and pattern of that unit with the idea of 'dividing'—the opposite, one would think, of 'handing'. Here are these six stanzas, in Russian and 'literal' English. (I omit my notes on diction, connotations, etc.)

2

. . . .

(Da, v chas, kogda poyezd podan,

Vy zhenshchinam, kak bokal,
pechal'nuyu chest' ukhoda

(Yes, at the-hour when the-train is-served,
You to-women, like a-goblet,
The-sorrowful honour of-departure

3

Vruchayete . . .)—Mozhet, bred?
Oslyshalsa? (Lzhets uchtiviy,
Lyubovnitse kak buket
Krovavuyu chest' razryva

Hand . . .)—Perhaps, delirium?
I-misheard? (Courteous liar,
To-your-lover like a-bouquet
The-bloody honour of-rift

4

Vruchayushchi . . .)—Vnyatno: slog
Za slogom, itak—prostimsa,

Skazalivy? (Kakplatok
V chas sladostnovo beschinstva

.

Handing . . .)(It's)-clear: syllable

After syllable, so—let's-say-goodbye,
You/said? (*Like a-handkerchief*
At the-hour of-voluptuous recklessness

5

Uronenny . . .)—Bitvy sei
Vy—Tsezar'. (O, vypad nagly!

Dropped . . .)—Of-this/battle
You-are Caesar. (O, insolent/thrust!

Protivniku—kak trofei,	*To-(your)-opponent—like a-trophy,*
Im otdannuyu zhe shpagu	*The very sabre that he surrendered*

6

Vruchat'!)—Prodolzhayet. (Zvon	*To-hand!)*—It-continues. (Sound
V ushakh ...)—Preklonyayus' dvazhdy:	In (my)-ears ...)I-bow twice:
Vpervye operezhon	For-the-first-time-I-am-forestalled
Vrazryve.—Vy eto kazhdoi?	In a-rift.—Do-you-(say) this to-every-(woman)?

7

Ne oprovergaite! Mest'	Don't deny-(it)! A-vengeance
Dostoinaya Lovelasa.	Worthy of-Lovelace.
Zhest, delayushchi vam chest',	*A-gesture doing you honour,*
A mne rzvodyashchi myaso	*But for-me dividing the-flesh*

8

Ot kosti.	*From the-bone.*

All subsequent instances of the dative case in this poem stand out strongly because of this established pattern: as, for example, the 'Do you say this to everyone?' in stanza 6; the later plea not to speak of their love to anyone coming after; and, especially, the final interchange about whether to give each other a parting gift such as a ring or a book.

Different syntactic patterns dominate other lyrics in the cycle. Their presence, as a fundamental structure, is typical of the whole of 'Poem of the End', and is a device which Tsvetaeva has elaborated with complete originality.

Angela Livingstone

Notes

We are keeping an eye on the girls

8   *kvass*: a common Russian drink, non-alcoholic, made from fermented rye bread.

Razin: Stenka Razin was a Cossack leader of the seventeenth-century peasant rebellion in Russia. According to legend, he sacrificed a Persian girl whom he loved to the river Volga.

No one has taken anything away

9   This poem is addressed to Osip Mandelstam (1892–1938); he and Tsvetaeva were lovers for a short while in 1916.

Derzhavin: (1743–1816) the most important Russian poet writing before Pushkin.

You throw back your head

10   Also written for Mandelstam, who recorded a similar excitement in walking about Moscow in his own poem 'With no confidence in miracles of redemption' (*Tristia*, 1922).

Where does this tenderness come from?

11   Again addressed to Mandelstam.

Today or tomorrow the snow will melt

13   Rogozhin: character in Dostoyevsky's novel *The Idiot*, who sets out to kill Prince Myshkin.

Verses about Moscow

14   I lift you up: the first lyric from this cycle is addressed to Tsvetaeva's daughter, Alya.

forty times forty [churches]: a phrase often used of Moscow.

Vagankovo: well-known cemetery in Moscow, where Tsvetaeva's parents were buried.

15   Strange and beautiful brother: the second lyric is addressed to Mandelstam, who lived in St Petersburg, and to whom Tsvetaeva offers her native city, Moscow.

Spassky gate/five cathedrals: in the Kremlin.

Inadvertent Joy: a wonder-working icon of the Virgin Mary, not far from the Kremlin.

Peter: Peter the Great (1689–1725) founded St Petersburg, which replaced Moscow as his capital.

126

17 Child Panteleimon: saint revered in the Orthodox Church, supposed to protect people's health.

Iversky heart: another wonder-working icon of the Virgin Mary, for which a special chapel was built, and which was taken to the city of Vladimir in 1812.

Poems for Akhmatova

23 Anna Akhmatova (1889–1966).

Ah!: in Russian '*akh*', the first syllable of the poet's name.

24 Tsarskoselsky: Akhmatova spent much of her youth in, and thereafter frequently revisited, the imperial town of Tsarskoe Selo, near St Petersburg.

Poems for Blok

26 Alexander Blok (1880–1921), Symbolist poet, with whom Tsvetaeva was never personally acquainted, although she met him briefly on two occasions.

five signs: in the old orthography (altered after the Revolution, but always appealing to Tsvetaeva) Blok's name was spelt with five letters—these four, plus a 'hard sign'.

spectre/knight/snow/wind: examples of images that deliberately recall images and words from poems by Blok himself.

28 Poem 3: the first two lines and the penultimate line of this poem are a re-phrasing of words from a well-known prayer sung in the Orthodox Church.

your river Neva: Blok's native city was St Petersburg. The first phrase of this poem '*U menya v Moskve*' could also be translated, to emphasize the contrast, 'In my Moscow'.

red calico of Kaluga: literally 'Kaluga native calico'. Tsvetaeva evokes a typical peasant scene at Tarusa, in Kaluga, where she spent her childhood summers in the family dacha.

30 Poem 9 is dated 9 May 1920, and Tsvetaeva notes on her manuscript: 'On the day when the powder cellars were blown up in the Khodynka and the window panes were shattered in the Polytechnic Museum, where Blok was reading.'

blue cloak: an image from Blok's poem '*O podvigakh, o doblesty-akh, o slave*', written in 1908 and addressed to his wife.

We shall call for the sun ... : referring to Blok's poem '*Golos iz khora*' (1910), with its lines: 'You will call for the sun's rising—/the sun will lie low' (in the version by Jon Stallworthy and Peter France).

Swans' Encampment

34 This is one lyric from a long cycle of poems written in Moscow between 1917–21, which was never published in Tsvetaeva's life-time. In many of them she adapts the lay of Prince Igor, and the tone of a lamenting Yaroslavna, to describe the heroic nobility of the White Army's self-sacrifice. When she returned to the Soviet Union in 1939 she left the ms at the University of Basel. It has been suggested that she was persuaded by accounts

127

of her husband, Sergei Efron's experiences in the White Army (which he found very different from the legendary heroes she describes) not to publish it. This is not so; only an accident, namely a quarrel with the Paris editors of *Latest News*, prevented the poems appearing there in 1928. Ironically, the quarrel arose out of Tsvetaeva's admiration for poetry written in the Soviet Union.

34 Ry-azan: the voice names a town near Moscow, and Tsvetaeva breaks the word, drawing out the long syllable to mime the accent of peasants who live there.

God help us   Smoke!

41 Written on 30 September 1922, shortly after Tsvetaeva and her daughter Alya joined Efron in Czechoslovakia.
necklace of coins: the note on p. 748 of the Moscow-Leningrad edition suggests the reference is to a doorman or hall-porter wearing many medals.

Ophelia: in Defence of the Queen

42 One of a run of epistolary poems; there is another written as if from Ophelia to Hamlet on the same date (28 February 1923).

Wherever you are I can reach you

43 the white book: Tsvetaeva means to deny that she has been reading 'black magic', or is a witch in the ordinary sense. She refers to the river Don (site of a White stand during the Civil War that she had commemorated in 'Swans' Encampment'), and has in mind the power given to her imagination by the long separation she endured then.

Wires

44 A note on p. 749 of the 1965 edition says: 'from a cycle of 10 poems . . . inspired by the correspondence with Pasternak which began in June 1922, soon after Tsvetaeva went abroad, and which continued for many years. Under Tsvetaeva's draft of no. 4 there is a note which later went into a letter to Pasternak: "Poems are the tracks by which I enter your soul. But your soul recedes and I get impatient, I jump ahead, blindly on the off chance, and then I wait in trepidation: will it turn my way?" . . .'
rigging: a number of puns in the Russian original make this a less conventional image than it might appear. 'Atlantic', for example, is contrasted with 'Pacific' meaning tranquil.
distance: again much word-play is lost in translation: 'receding' contains a syllable '*dal*' meaning distance, and '*zhal*' (pity) picks this up as a rhyme.
still implored: the Russian makes clear that it is the distance that is being implored by the voices.

Sahara

46 This poem is written at the height of Tsvetaeva's passionate correspondence with the twenty-year-old critic, Alexander Bakhrakh, whom she had never

met, but upon whose loving support she depended so strongly that a break in his flow of letters brought her almost to collapse.

Poem of the Mountain

59 After helping to settle her daughter Alya in a boarding-school in Moravia during August 1923, Tsvetaeva took a flat alone on the wooded hill at the centre of Prague. During the autumn of 1923 she had the most passionate love affair of her life, with Konstantin Borisovich Rodzevitch, regarded by the émigrés of Prague as a White Officer, though he had in fact fought with the Red Navy.

62 Hagar: Abraham's slave and concubine, who bore him a son, Ishmael, was sent away at the insistence of Abraham's wife and went to live in the Arabian desert.

63 twelve apostles: Tsvetaeva is probably referring to the clock tower on the Old Town Square in Prague, where the twelve apostles appear as the hour strikes.

Poem of the End

67 There are fourteen poems in this cycle (some divided into two or three lyrics); the eleventh poem is not translated.

The love affair with Rodzevitch was over by December 1923, and this poem records exactly how she learns of his decision to end their relationship, as they meet, walk about the city of Prague with its many bridges, and talk over café tables.

69 a window under the roof . . . /it is burning?: a rephrasing of lines from a poem by Blok.

who shall I tell my sorrow: words from the Psalter.

70 Semiramis: Assyrian princess (c. 800 B.C.) famous for her hanging gardens, one of the Seven Wonders of the World.

71 Star of Malta: emblem of a medieval knightly order.

72 powder/made by Berthold Schwartz: gunpowder.

75 The stamp left on your heart/would be the ring on your hand: an allusion to the Song of Songs (8:6): 'Set me as a seal upon thine heart . . .'

85 Khlebnikov: Russian Futurist poet.

88 Marinkas: Marinka is a diminutive of Marina, a common Polish name (and well-known to Russians from the princess in Pushkin's *Boris Godunov*).

The Ratcatcher

93 These are three sections from a long narrative poem which follows the story of the Pied Piper. It is marked throughout with a disgust for material well-being, so that the abundance in the town is felt as a direct cause of the plague of rats. In later sections of the poem the burghers give the flute-player a contemptuous dressing-down on the use of his art. D. S. Mirsky wrote of *The Ratcatcher*: '. . . it is not only a verbal structure that is astounding in its richness and harmony, it is also a serious "political" . . . and "ethical"

satire.' Tsvetaeva began writing the poem in Vshenory in early 1925, and completed it in Paris in November that year.

96 poods: Russian measure.

Poems to a Son

100 Georgy returned to Russia with Tsvetaeva in 1939, to join his father and sister. When they were arrested he lived with his mother until they were evacuated to Yelabuga. After Tsvetaeva died, he left to join the army and died, still in his teens, in the defence of Moscow.

Homesickness

101 Kamchatka: far-eastern Siberian peninsula, sometimes invoked in the sense of 'back of beyond'.

Epitaph

104 These poems were written for N. P. Gronsky, a young poet killed in a street accident when he was twenty-four. Tsvetaeva had been close to him as a young boy of eighteen in Meudon, and continued to value his poetry highly after they stopped seeing one another.

Desk

109 Three lyrics from a sequence of six.

110 thirty years: the lyrics were written between 1933 and 1935, and Tsvetaeva must have had in mind her very earliest attempts at poetry.

Bus

113 Easter toys: on Palm Sunday most Russian towns held markets at which sweets, trinkets, and small devils and cherubim were commonly sold.

114 A moist, wood-twig smoke of green: although this verse appears to be another draft of the previous one, both appear in the Moscow-Leningrad edition.

115 Nebuchadnezzar: cf. Daniel, 4:31–3.

119 thief: there is multiple punning on the idea of pillaging as a form of (literal) 'ripping-off', or fleecing, throughout the passage.

Poems to Czechoslovakia

121 Tsvetaeva was thinking of the region known to her as 'Chekhia' in the country we have recently called Czechoslovakia.

Vary/Tatras: Karlovy vary (Karlsbad), a famous spa in western Czechoslovakia. By mentioning it along with 'Tatry', the Tatras, mountain ranges in the eastern part of that country, Tsvetaeva means to emphasize that the Germans took the whole of the country, and all the pleasures that if offered.

they won: 'won' in Russian can also mean 'took'.

spittle: the original poem is headed by a sentence from the newspapers of March 1939: 'The Czechs went up to the Germans and spat'.

130

122 give back to God his ticket: this seems to be a reference to Ivan Karamazov
     (in Dostoyevsky's *Brothers Karamazov*), who defiantly offered back to God
     his entrance ticket to Heaven so long as Heaven is built upon or despite the
     suffering of children on earth.

FOR THE BEST IN PAPERBACKS, LOOK FOR THE

In every corner of the world, on every subject under the sun, Penguin represents quality and variety—the very best in publishing today.

For complete information about books available from Penguin—including Penguin Classics, Penguin Compass, and Puffins—and how to order them, write to us at the appropriate address below. Please note that for copyright reasons the selection of books varies from country to country.

In the United States: Please write to *Penguin Group (USA), P.O. Box 12289 Dept. B, Newark, New Jersey 07101-5289* or call 1-800-788-6262.

In the United Kingdom: Please write to *Dept. EP, Penguin Books Ltd, Bath Road, Harmondsworth, West Drayton, Middlesex UB7 0DA.*

In Canada: Please write to *Penguin Books Canada Ltd, 10 Alcorn Avenue, Suite 300, Toronto, Ontario M4V 3B2.*

In Australia: Please write to *Penguin Books Australia Ltd, P.O. Box 257, Ringwood, Victoria 3134.*

In New Zealand: Please write to *Penguin Books (NZ) Ltd, Private Bag 102902, North Shore Mail Centre, Auckland 10.*

In India: Please write to *Penguin Books India Pvt Ltd, 11 Panchsheel Shopping Centre, Panchsheel Park, New Delhi 110 017.*

In the Netherlands: Please write to *Penguin Books Netherlands bv, Postbus 3507, NL-1001 AH Amsterdam.*

In Germany: Please write to *Penguin Books Deutschland GmbH, Metzlerstrasse 26, 60594 Frankfurt am Main.*

In Spain: Please write to *Penguin Books S. A., Bravo Murillo 19, 1° B, 28015 Madrid.*

In Italy: Please write to *Penguin Italia s.r.l., Via Benedetto Croce 2, 20094 Corsico, Milano.*

In France: Please write to *Penguin France, Le Carré Wilson, 62 rue Benjamin Baillaud, 31500 Toulouse.*

In Japan: Please write to *Penguin Books Japan Ltd, Kaneko Building, 2-3-25 Koraku, Bunkyo-Ku, Tokyo 112.*

In South Africa: Please write to *Penguin Books South Africa (Pty) Ltd, Private Bag X14, Parkview, 2122 Johannesburg.*